This book is dedicated to my grandmother,
Hettie Bell, in whose scullery we spent many happy
times as a family, watching and learning.

Kind were the voices I used to hear
Round such a fireside,
Speaking the mother tongue old and dear ...

Alexander Nicolson, nineteenth century Scottish poet[1]

THE
SCULLERY

Recipes from an
Ulster-Scots heritage

THE
SCULLERY
Recipes from an
Ulster-Scots heritage

DIANE HOY

Published 2011 by
Colourpoint Books
Colourpoint House, Jubilee Business Park
Jubilee Road, Newtownards, BT23 4YH
Tel: 028 9182 6339
Fax: 028 9182 1900
E-mail: info@colourpoint.co.uk
Web: www.colourpoint.co.uk

First Edition
First Impression

Designed by April Sky Design, Newtownards
Tel: 028 9182 7195
Web: www.aprilsky.co.uk

Printed by W&G Baird, Antrim

ISBN 978-1-906578-92-3

Explore, discover and buy other titles on Northern Ireland
subjects at BooksNI.com – the online bookshop for Northern Ireland

CONTENTS

THE AUTHOR

Photograph courtesy Waddell Media
– *Paul & Nick's Big Food Trip.*

Diane Hoy works part-time for Queen's University Belfast, Northern Ireland, and is a part-time author. She lives in Belfast with her family and spends most weekends at the family caravan in Cloughey, County Down on the beautiful Ards Peninsula.

Educated at Methodist College Belfast, Diane originally worked in the library service for sixteen years, eight of which were spent as branch librarian in Braniel Library, Belfast. An enthusiastic amateur cook, this was followed by forays into the catering and hospitality industry, at one time working as a trainee kitchen manager in a Scottish hotel on the banks of Loch Lomond, before returning to Northern Ireland to open a coffee shop in Belfast and, several years later, a small café in the Lisburn area of County Antrim.

In later years, she has worked in a variety of administrative posts culminating in four years as Development Officer for the Ulster-Scots Heritage Council. She was Chair of the Belfast Ulster-Scots Festival in 2005 and 2006, Chair of the Ulster-Scots Border Counties Gaitherin in 2006, and, keen to promote the importance of libraries in her community's culture, designed and organised exhibition launches with each of Northern Ireland's five education and library boards between 2004 and 2006. In 2007, she was invited by ITV newsreader and journalist, Fiona Armstrong, to organise and accompany a group of Ulster-Scots dancers and musicians to visit Scotland and participate in the annual Clan Armstrong Gather in Langholm, and the annual Clan Gathering in Dumfries.

Diane has published an article on Ulster-Scots cooking in *Oot an Aboot*, the Ulster-Scots Agency's magazine, and appears in a forthcoming Ulster Television series on Ulster-Scots cooking featuring the celebrity chefs, Paul Rankin from Northern Ireland, and Nick Nairn from Scotland. This is her first cookery book.

ACKNOWLEDGMENTS

I would like to thank the following people who helped me turn a dream into a reality: Malcolm, Rachel and Jacky at Colourpoint Books for their support, advice and professionalism; my brother, Jeff, for helping me with digital photography; and my family and friends at home and abroad, not only for recalling and providing many of the recipes, but also for their encouragement and steadfast belief in me.

AUTHOR'S NOTE

Fair faa ye, yin an aa!

Hello or welcome, everyone!

Background

This is a book I promised to write several years ago after many unsuccessful attempts to purchase or borrow any dedicated Ulster-Scots cookery books through a bookstore or library. To date, very little has been written on the subject so in early autumn 2007 I decided that the time had come. I set up an office at home, joined a creative writing course, and began my research. I do not claim to be a culinary expert, rather my intention is that this book be read as an introduction to the traditional and contemporary ingredients and recipes of the Ulster-Scots, using personal recollections, historical facts, and relevant snippets of Ulster-Scots and Scots poetry. Throughout my research, I found plenty of material for an historical Ulster-Scots cookery book – perhaps a future project!

My family's Ulster-Scots connection is mainly through my maternal grandparents – the Bells – who hailed from Antrim and Ballycastle. My mother's cousin, Neville Wilson, researched the origins of the family several years ago, uncovering a trail leading back to my great-great-great-great grandfather, David Bell, who resided in Auchtermuchty, Fifeshire, Scotland. The clan was traced throughout Scotland until circa 1899 when my great-grandfather, James Bell, came to Ulster, married my great-grandmother who was from Castleblaney, Co Monaghan, and settled in Belfast. Someday I plan to do the same for the Hoy clan – thought to have originated in the Orkneys (the island of 'Hoy' is the second largest) and the Scottish Borders, the earliest reference being 1483.

In my long and varied career, I was a librarian for sixteen years and trained as a kitchen manager in a Scottish hotel before returning to Belfast to set up a coffee shop. In recent years, I've worked as Development Officer for the Ulster-Scots Language Society and the Ulster-Scots Heritage Council.

I found that the idea of a straightforward recipe book had instead become a trawl through childhood memories, especially those of watching my granny in her scullery preparing family meals. Hence this book has resulted in the resurrection of recipes passed down through the family, collected from friends at home and abroad, or re-created from memory as the original recipe is long gone from my scrapbooks. It's a combination of recipes which I've either loved or loathed but all of which hold a special meaning for me.

Language

You will discover that on the odd occasion I use words or phrases in the Ulster-Scots language which some of you may be familiar with. Throughout my childhood I grew up listening to dialogue regularly spoken in our family without actually realising where it originated. It wasn't until I began to appreciate my cultural and linguistic heritage that I realised these words were common to a large percentage of the population, especially those Ulster-Scots living in rural areas of Counties Antrim and Down, North-East Londonderry and East Donegal.

Ulster-Scots is a variant of the Scots language, the tongue of the Lowland Scots who settled in Ulster in the early 1600s. Both languages are Germanic in origin. Ulster-Scots is officially recognised as a language by the European Charter for Regional or Minority Languages and ratified by the UK government in March 2001.

Due to our rich literary heritage, I've incorporated relevant excerpts of poetry written by traditional Ulster-Scots poets known as *The Rhyming Weavers*, James Orr, Robert Huddleston, Samuel Thomson and Hugh Porter being the most well-known. They were nineteenth century working class people – weavers, farmers, school masters – living in rural communities from which they drew their inspiration and writing in the Ulster-Scots vernacular in which they spoke on a daily basis. I've also used excerpts from Scots poems including those of Rabbie Burns; Ulster street rhymes, many learned through skipping games in my youth; and some of the best-known Ulster-Scots poets of today including James Fenton and Charlie Gillen.

Weights and Measures

I've tried to ensure that the measurements are in metric as well as imperial and that a standard table is used throughout. Many of our family recipes were handwritten (usually on the back on an envelope!) and imperial weights were, and are, used to this day. Many were scribbled down without exact measurements, leaving the cook with just the general gist of how the recipe was to be made. Over the last few years, after gaining more confidence in home cooking, I have found that I depend less on sticking to the actual written recipe and more on using my own initiative as there are ingredients which I, or my guests, don't like, can't eat, or I simply can't find in the shops. The exception is in home baking when it is important to stick to the recipe – as I've found to my cost!

Healthy Eating

Ulster-Scots cooking tends towards using the produce of the farms, orchards, rivers, and seas, therefore the ingredients are local, fresh and wholesome, and cooked in a variety of ways to enhance the natural flavour. I have used butter, oil, cheese and cream in a lot of my recipes because they enrich the taste, but please feel free to substitute these for a low-fat alternative.

Portions

All recipes serve four people unless indicated otherwise.

O Lord,
Wha blessed the loaves and fishes,
Look doon upon these twa bit dishes,
And tho' the tatties be but sma',
Lord, mak them plenty for us a'.
But if our stomachs they do fill
'Twill be another miracle.

A Scots Grace (Anon)[2]

INTRODUCTION

Hae ye na plenty
O' what's haelsome and dainty?
Wheat bread, meat an' mil, an' a' that;
An' may, when you please,
Eat an' drink at your ease,
Then, what the deil was ye be at?

David Bruce, an Ulster-Scot-American poet (c. 1760–1830)[3]

Little has been written about Ulster-Scots cooking, traditional or contemporary. Ask an Ulster man or woman what constitutes Ulster-Scots fare and they will most likely mention the Ulster Fry or stew. Starchy bread and potatoes may be considered the staple diet of an Ulster-Scot but this is not necessarily the case, as I hope to prove!

Very few recipes are invented – most are modern adaptations of traditional dishes. A trawl through historical cookery books can often reveal similar recipes with different names. National cuisines vary from country to country, although it is interesting to discover several cuisines claiming ownership of the same dish, which all goes to prove that the diversity and pedigree of many cultures naturally produces a shared culinary heritage.

In an historical sense, Ulster-Scots food is a combination of Ulster, Scottish, and English styles of cooking, a reflection of the early Scottish and English settlers during the Hamilton and Montgomery Settlement of 1606 and James VI's Plantation of Ulster in 1610. The immigration of the French Huguenots to Ulster in the seventeenth century and the emigration of the Ulster-Scots to the New World in the eighteenth century, introduced a European and South East American influence.

The early Ulster-Scots were a thran and hardy bunch, creating a new life for themselves amidst a barren land desolated by war and famine – a far cry from the prosperous, fertile land imagined. In the beginning, they struggled to survive but did so through hard work and successful harvests during the first few years. They also helped to establish modern farming and agricultural methods, and today their Ulster-Scots descendants are predominantly from a rural as well as a seafaring background.

In the seventeenth century people ate according to the seasons and what was available – no fridge freezers and popping round to the local supermarket in those days! Animals would have been hunted for their meat; fish caught from the local rivers and seas; mushrooms, nuts and berries gathered from woodland areas; and porridge, oatcakes and breads made using hand-operated querns or water-powered mills to grind the grain.

The beginning of the Industrial Revolution in the eighteenth century saw the growth and development of corn mills producing ground oats, barley and wheat. The potato, which had been introduced into Ireland during the seventeenth century, was now considered a staple food, especially during the winter months, when one of its many uses was as a thickening agent for soups and stews. It thrived in the rainy summer months and mild climate. From the eighteenth century onwards, a wider range of fruit and vegetables was also available, and a meal of meat and vegetables was considered incomplete unless accompanied by the potato. Popular imports resulted in sugar replacing honey as a sweetener and tea replacing ale as the common beverage.

In the nineteenth century, the growth of the Industrial Revolution saw hard manual labour in rural communities such as crop gathering, butter churning and milking by hand gradually replaced with food processing and preservation techniques. Fresh meat was more readily available – and therefore more affordable – to the working classes and poultry was reared on a larger scale. Grocers were established in the larger towns enabling a wider choice of foodstuff and outdoor markets thrived in rural towns and villages. The Victorian building hosting Belfast's famous St George's Market was built between 1890 and 1896 and continues to sell fresh, local produce at its Friday and Saturday markets today.

In the twentieth century, due to trade route expansion and new developments in food preservation, especially that of 'freezing', the importing and exporting of food from around the world changed our relationship with food. The first supermarket was introduced into Northern Ireland and fast food outlets began to spring up around the country.

Today, wheat, oats and barley are some of the home-grown cereals used in the production of our wide variety of breads – soda bread (*farls,* from the Scots word 'fardel'), potato bread (*fadge),* wheaten bread, treacle bread, scones, pancakes, fruit loaves, and the malt bread, Veda. Veda was invented by the Scot, Robert Graham in Gleneagles in 1904 and Northern Ireland is the only country in the United Kingdom still making it today.

Ulster pork, beef, lamb and poultry are of the highest quality from animals reared in verdant pastures, the grass made lush with abundant rain. Salmon, trout, eels, cod, skate, plaice, herrings, mackerel, lobsters, prawns, oysters and mussels, locally caught in our seas, lakes and rivers, offer a wide choice to the discerning chef.

Dairy farms produce milk, butter, cream and yoghurt, and Glastry Farm in County Down and Hoy's Farmhouse in County Antrim make their own ice cream from local dairy herds. Free range eggs are readily available to purchase fresh from local farms, and local cheeses such as Ballybrie and Ballyblue soft cheeses and Dromona cheddar, all from County Tyrone, and Coleraine cheddar from County Londonderry, are now exported to an international market.

Orchard fruit such as pears, plums and County Armagh's famous Bramley apples, and the soft fruit from Counties Antrim and Down like the raspberry, strawberry, tayberry, gooseberry, red and blackcurrants, are popular in light summer puddings, autumn jams and chutneys. The wide variety of tuber and root vegetables such as the Comber potato from County Down and rhubarb grown near the banks of Lough Neagh, with cauliflower, cabbage, carrot, swede, parsnip, pamphrey, mushrooms, onion and beetroot, all thrive in the rich agricultural heartland of the Ulster-Scots.

Contemporary Ulster-Scots cooking remains flavoursome and uncomplicated, taking advantage of locally produced meat and poultry, fish, fruit and vegetables and cooking these in a variety of delicious and healthy ways. The main emphasis is on fresh, simplistic, wholesome fare.

CHAPTER 1

Whun tha Slabbers are Trippin' Ye!

––––––⬥⬥⬥––––––

An eating horse ne'er foundered.
It is a healthy sign when people eat well.

Scots saying[4]

I've kicked off the first chapter with food that
has tickled my taste buds over the years, those
tried and tested recipes which have become my
favourites. In other words, if set before me, *tha
slabbers wud be trippin' me!*

Tha Ulster Fry

Who hasn't heard of our national dish! As a child I hated the very smell of a fry, but now I look forward to coming down to a fried breakfast whilst on holiday – be it an English, Scottish, or Irish version. Here in Ulster, the main ingredient would be fried bread – usually potato bread and soda bread – although fried pancake and wheaten are also popular. Vegetable roll is added if we have the fry at dinner time purely because we find it a bit heavy for breakfast. The vegetable roll is a tasty mixture of finely minced meat (usually brisket), onions, leeks, carrots, white pepper and herbs usually rolled in waxed paper and ready sliced. It can be bought in any good butcher's shop or supermarket. If you've never had an Ulster fry, you haven't lived. This is our family version.

Ingredients:

Free-range eggs

Ulster bacon (I prefer unsmoked back bacon)

Good quality Ulster pork or beef sausages

Vegetable roll

Potato Bread (see following recipe)

Soda Farl (see following recipe)

Mushrooms

Tomatoes

Oil for frying

Preparation

You'll need a large, heavy-based frying pan or multi-cooker.

Heat oil until hot, add sausages, vegetable roll and bacon and fry until cooked right through. Place onto heated plate and keep warm under grill.

Place bread in pan and fry until golden on both sides – the fat from the meat will taste the bread. Place bread on warmed plate under grill and add tomatoes and mushrooms to the pan, tossing over a high heat until they cook (add butter if pan is too dry). Place these under grill to keep warm.

Add more oil to the pan until the pan is half full. When oil is heated through, time to fry the eggs. Crack the eggs into the pan, wait until white is thick and cooked and baste the egg yolk with the oil until cooked to your preference.

When all ingredients have been cooked, plate up and get stuck in!

Soda Farls

My granny would simply have used a floured worktop surface and her hands to mix these ingredients, but I'll leave it up to you! The more traditional method of cooking is to heat a griddle pan or hot plate until flour sprinkled over the top browns slightly. The mixture should be divided into 'rounds' and baked on both sides for 5–10 minutes until cooked through. For this recipe, I'm using a conventional oven.

Ingredients:

8oz/225g plain flour

½ tsp baking soda

½ tsp salt

¼ pint/140ml buttermilk

1 egg, lightly beaten

Preparation:

Sieve together flour, baking soda and salt in a bowl.

Make a well in the centre and add the egg and buttermilk, mixing in a little at a time until a soft consistency is reached. You may need less or more buttermilk depending on consistency – don't feel you have to use the exact amount stated if the mixture is getting too wet!

*Using your hands, shape the mixture into a round shape and turn out onto a floured surface. Make a cross shape on the top of the loaf with a knife, dividing it into quarters or **farls** (from the Scots word 'fardel').*

Bake in a pre-heated oven at 400°F, 200°C, Gas mark 6 for 25–30 minutes. You'll know the loaf is cooked by tapping on the underside – a hollow sound should be heard.

Oaten Potato Bread (Fadge)

Potato bread, or *fadge*, is traditionally a potato and flour mixture but this recipe adds oatmeal to give it an interesting texture and flavour.

Ingredients:

8oz/225g cold mashed potato
Pinch of salt
2 *gowpins* (handfuls) plain flour
3 *gowpins* (handfuls) medium oatmeal

Preparation:

Heat a griddle pan or hot plate until flour sprinkled over the top browns slightly.

On a floured worktop, knead potato, salt, flour and oatmeal together until well combined. Roll into four farls (quarters) and sprinkle with flour.

Cook on a hot griddle for approximately 5 minutes on each side until cooked through.

Wheaten Bread

I prefer my wheaten to be moist rather than *brückly* and buttermilk helps to do just that.

Ingredients:

1lb/450g soda bread flour

8oz/225g wheatmeal flour

8oz/225g wholemeal flour

4oz/115g margarine

2oz/55g granulated sugar

2 tsp baking soda

1 tsp salt

1½ pints (850ml) buttermilk

Preparation:

Mix all the flours into a large bowl. Rub margarine into the flour, and add all other DRY ingredients. Lastly, add enough buttermilk to form a soft consistency.

Divide the mixture into two and put each loaf into a greased and floured 2lb/900g loaf tin.

Bake in a pre-heated oven at 375°F, 190°C or Gas mark 5 for 40 minutes. When cool, slice and eat buttered with homemade jam.

Buttermilk Pancakes

Pancakes are easy to make but are always best eaten the same day. They can be eaten cold with butter and jam or fried as part of an Ulster Fry. Larger, thinner pancakes can be used as a dessert when filled with soft fruit and whipped cream, then folded over and dusted with icing sugar.

Ingredients:

8oz/225g plain flour

2 tbsp caster sugar

½ tsp salt

½ tsp baking soda

1 egg, beaten

Buttermilk

Preparation:

Sieve flour, sugar, salt and baking soda into a large bowl. Add beaten egg and mix through. Add enough buttermilk to make a dropping consistency.

Heat a large greased frying pan until very hot and drop in spoonfuls of the pancake mixture (size of spoon dependent on what size you want your pancakes). When bubbles appear on the mixture, turn over and cook on other side. When golden and cooked through, lift onto plate and serve immediately with butter and squeezed lemon juice or maple syrup.

Mars Bar and Veda Sarnies

Veda bread was invented by a Scotsman, Robert Graham in 1904 and our wee country is the only one in the UK still making it. My mum sometimes gave me a special treat by making these for my school packed lunch. I could hardly concentrate on lessons waiting for the lunch bell to sound!

Ingredients:

1 Mars Bar

4 rounds of Veda bread, buttered

Preparation:

Slice Mars thinly and spread over two of the slices. Top with remaining slices and squish down until butter oozes out the sides. Sink teeth into sandwich and relish!

Granny's Chip Butties

My granny and mum make the best chips I've ever tasted. Granny used lard for frying them, not very acceptable in today's healthy eating climate but believe me, they tasted so much better. Goose or duck fat, if you can get it, also creates that extra special flavour.

Ingredients:

Potatoes, waxy are best (allow approximately 1 large potato per person)

Bread (2 rounds per person, preferably white pan or plain loaf)

Butter

Salt

Goose/duck fat (or sunflower oil)

Preparation:

Wash and peel potatoes. Slice into chips and deep fat fry in oil for about 5–10 minutes depending on thickness. Don't overload the pan or the chips won't crisp up, better to cook them in batches.

While chips are cooking, butter the bread. Drain the chips, place on one round of buttered bread, season to taste (you can add vinegar, tomato ketchup, brown sauce, mayonnaise – the list is endless!) and top with the second round. Eat – and enjoy the warm butter dribbling down your chin – all part of the experience!

Pan-Fried Fillet of Beef with Mushroom Sauce

I'm not a steak lover but this is what I'd choose for a very special occasion. It's the most expensive cut of beef and deliciously tender, so should be the centrepiece of the meal without complicated or overpowering accompaniments. I like to eat it with homemade chips and this earthy mushroom sauce served on the side – to dip the chips in!

Ingredients:

1 slice of fillet beef per person
Sea salt and black pepper
Olive oil for frying

Sauce:
8oz/225g mushrooms, coarsely chopped
3 shallots, peeled and finely chopped
2oz/55g butter
1 tbsp olive oil
1 tsp cornflour
¼ pt/140ml double cream
Seasoning

Preparation:

Season both sides of the beef. Heat the oil in a large pan and when hot, add the fillets, cooking both sides for approximately 3–4 minutes or until cooked to your liking. Remove from the pan and leave to rest for a few minutes.

Heat the butter and oil in a large frying pan, add the shallots and cook for 3 minutes. Add the mushrooms and cook on a low heat for 2 minutes. Season, add the flour and cook for 1 minute. Stir in the cream and cook for 3–5 minutes over a low heat until the sauce begins to thicken. Serve in a sauce boat.

Good friends, let me advise you all,
Wee Fish or Flesh, of Mutton Spaull,
We' Beef, cram well yer Money-saul,
Then never shrink,
Or fear yer **** shou'd be mad cald
We muckle Drink.

William Starratt of Strabane, the Crochan Bard (eighteenth century)[5]

Savoury Mince Pie and Baked Beans

Wednesday was my favourite day at primary school because my mum would have visited a wee bakery opposite the Ormeau Park in Belfast and brought home the most delicious savoury mince pies (similar in size to the sweet mince pies we get at Christmas) which we'd have served hot with baked beans for lunch. Alas the bakery and pies are long gone, so I've chosen my own recipe for a large savoury mince pie. I find that a mixture of soft margarine and lard works very well in producing a crisp pastry.

Ingredients:

Shortcrust Pastry:

8oz/225g plain flour

Pinch of salt

2oz/55g soft margarine

2oz/55g lard

2–3 tbsp cold water

Beaten egg to glaze

Filling:

8oz/225g minced beef

1 small onion, chopped finely

1 small carrot, chopped into small cubes

1 garlic clove, chopped finely

1 tbsp tomato ketchup

1 tsp Worcester sauce

Seasoning

Oil for frying

Preparation:

Grease a 9in/23cm pie plate. Sift flour and salt into a bowl. Cut margarine and lard into cubes and gradually rub into flour until mixture resembles fine breadcrumbs. Add enough water to form a soft dough. Divide into two and wrap in cling film. Leave in fridge for 30 minutes to rest.

Pour oil into a large saucepan with the garlic and heat slowly, making sure the garlic does not become burned. Add the onion and half cover with a lid, reducing heat to a gentle simmer. Cook until the onion is softened. Add the minced beef and brown all over. Add the carrot, sauces and seasoning, and mix well. Replace the lid and simmer for 30 minutes until the meat is cooked. Leave until the meat is cold before placing on the pastry.

In the meantime, roll each pastry half out on a floured surface. Use one half to cover the bottom of the greased pie dish, and add the cold meat on top. Dampen the pastry edge with cold water before covering it with the remaining pastry half. Trim, seal and pinch the edges, then prick the top of the pastry before glazing it with the beaten egg.

Cook in a pre-heated oven at 350°F, 180°C, Gas mark 4 for approximately 30–35 minutes. Serve hot with baked beans!

My Aunt's Trio of Vol-au-Vents

My Aunt Anthea would make these mouth watering treats on special family occasions when a finger buffet of tasty treats was the order of the day. Vol-au-vents are terrifically versatile for using up leftover food and these are three of her favourite fillings. If making all of the fillings, make a large quantity of the white sauce, divide it amongst three bowls and add the separate fillings.

CHICKEN AND PEACH

Ingredients:

12 small vol-au-vent cases

1oz/30g butter or margarine

1oz/30g plain flour

½pt/280ml milk

Seasoning

8oz/225g cooked chicken, finely chopped

2 peaches, chopped (or small tin peaches, chopped)

Preparation:

Cook the vol-au-vents according to the maker's instructions.

Make the white sauce by melting the butter in a saucepan and adding the flour. Stir over a medium heat for 1 minute until the flour is cooked. Gradually add the milk, stirring continuously over a medium heat until the milk is blended and the sauce begins to thicken. Season to taste and add the chicken and peaches.

Fill the cases with the mixture and put back in the oven for 5–10 minutes to ensure the filling is hot enough to serve.

SALMON AND PARSLEY

As above, but replace the chicken and peaches with two cooked medium salmon fillets (or one small tin of salmon, drained and bones removed) and a tablespoon of chopped parsley.

MUSHROOM AND SHERRY

As above, but replace the chicken and peaches with 4oz/115g of sliced, cooked mushrooms and one tablespoon of dry sherry.

Scones

I hate plain scones, so these are recipes using the scone base but with different flavours added.

LEMON AND SULTANA

Ingredients:

8oz/225g plain flour

1 tsp baking powder

½ tsp salt

1 egg

2oz/55g butter

1oz/30g caster sugar

A little buttermilk

2oz/55g sultanas

1 tsp lemon juice and rind of a lemon

Preparation:

Sieve the flour, salt, and baking powder together in a large bowl. Rub in the butter and when mixture resembles breadcrumbs, add sugar, sultanas, lemon juice and rind. Beat the egg and add to the mixture with enough buttermilk to make a medium soft dough.

Turn out onto a floured worktop and roll out to about ½ inch/1½ cm thick. Cut into round shapes, place on baking tray, brush with beaten egg and bake in a pre-heated oven at 425°F, 220°C, Gas mark 7 for 12–15 minutes.

CINNAMON AND RAISIN

Ingredients:

8oz/225g plain flour

1 tsp baking powder

½ tsp salt

1 egg

2oz/55g butter

1oz/30g caster sugar

A little buttermilk

2oz/55g raisins

1 tsp cinnamon

Preparation:

Follow instructions for Lemon and Sultana Scones but replace the lemon juice and the rind with cinnamon, and the sultanas with raisins!

CHERRY AND ALMOND

Ingredients:

8oz/225g plain flour

1 tsp baking powder

½ tsp salt

1 egg

2oz/55g butter

1oz/30g caster sugar

A little buttermilk

2oz/55g glacé cherries

Few drops almond essence

Preparation:

Follow instructions for Lemon and Sultana Scones but replace the lemon juice and the rind with almond essence, and the sultanas with cherries!

DATE AND WHEATEN

Ingredients:

4oz/115g plain flour

4oz/115g wholemeal flour

1 tsp baking powder

½ tsp salt

1 egg

2oz/55g butter

1oz/30g caster sugar

A little buttermilk

2oz/55g stoned and pre-soaked dates

Preparation:

Follow instructions for Lemon and Sultana Scones but take out the lemon juice and the rind, and replace the sultanas with dates!

MARS BAR SCONES

Ingredients:

8oz/225g plain flour

1 tsp baking powder

½ tsp salt

1 egg

2oz/55g butter

1oz/30g caster sugar

A little buttermilk

1 Mars Bar, chopped into small pieces

Preparation:

Follow instructions for Lemon and Sultana Scones but take out the lemon juice and the rind, and replace sultanas with Mars Bar pieces! These will melt during cooking to leave a yummy, gooey scone to mak yer teeth rin wätter!

SPICED TREACLE SCONES

Ingredients:

8oz/225g plain flour

1 tsp baking powder

½ tsp salt

1oz/30g caster sugar

1 tsp mixed spice

2oz/55g butter

2 tbsp treacle

A little buttermilk

1 egg

Preparation:

Sieve the flour, salt, and baking powder together in a large bowl. Add sugar and spice. Heat the butter with the treacle and pour into the centre, mixing well. Add enough buttermilk to make a medium soft dough.

Turn out onto a floured worktop and roll out to about ½ inch/1½ cm thick. Cut into round shapes, place on baking tray, brush with beaten egg and bake in a pre-heated oven at 425°F, 220°C, Gas mark 7 for 12–15 minutes.

My Aunt Jane's Tea Loaf

A traditional boiled loaf from Aunt Jane's wee shop in the well-known Ulster street song should be bursting with fruit infused in Punjana tea – a tea importing and blending company founded in Belfast in 1896.

Ingredients:

4oz/115g sultanas

4oz/115g raisins

2oz/55g cherries

4oz/115g soft brown sugar

5oz/140g butter

¼ pt/140ml strong, cold Punjana tea

8oz/225g self-raising flour

1 tsp mixed spice

2 eggs, lightly beaten

Preparation:

Steep fruit, sugar, spice and butter in the cold tea for 15–20 minutes. Add the beaten eggs to the fruit mixture. Sieve flour and add to the mixture ensuring that everything is well mixed through. Pour into a greased 2lb/900g loaf tin and bake in a pre-heated oven at 350°F, 180°C, Gas mark 4 for 1 hour. Test if cooked by inserting a skewer – if clean on removal, cake should be cooked. Turn out onto a wire rack to cool. Serve sliced and buttered.

My Aunt Jane, she called me in,
She gave me tea out of her wee tin.
Half a bap, sugar on the top,
Three black balls out of her wee shop.

Traditional Ulster Street Song[6]

Treacle Bread

Whenever I think of sticky black treacle (known as 'molasses' in the USA), it reminds me of the free treacle tarts offered up by the creepy Child-Catcher in Ian Fleming's Chitty-Chitty-Bang-Bang! Its main use in Ulster and Scottish cookery is in sweet dishes – treacle tart, treacle scones, or in this instance, treacle bread, a wonderfully, sticky fruit bread.

Ingredients:

4oz/115g plain flour

6oz/170g wholemeal flour

2oz/55g porridge oats

2oz/55g soft brown sugar

1 tsp salt

1 tsp baking soda

½oz/15g butter

1 egg, beaten

2 dessert spoons treacle

A little buttermilk

2oz/55g sultanas

2oz/55g raisins

2oz/55g stoned, pre-soaked dates

Preparation:

Mix together flour, oats, sugar, salt, and baking soda in a large bowl. Rub in butter, then add fruit. Make a well in the centre and add the beaten egg, treacle and enough buttermilk to make a dropping consistency. Pour into greased tin and bake in a pre-heated oven at 350°F, 180°C, Gas mark 4 for 40–45 minutes.

Chocolate and Strawberry Meringue

This is my favourite dessert of all time! If you have a sweet tooth, this is the cake to *mak yer teeth rin water* with its combination of fresh strawberries and chocolate!

Ingredients:

6 egg whites

12oz/340g caster sugar

3oz/85g ground almonds

6oz/170g soft butter or margarine

10oz/285g icing sugar

3oz/85g melted milk chocolate

Small punnet fresh Ulster strawberries

½pt/280ml double cream

Preparation:

Whisk the egg whites until stiff. Continue whisking whilst gradually adding half of the caster sugar until the mixture becomes glossy. Fold in the rest of the caster sugar and the ground almonds. Line three 9inch/23cm sandwich tins with greaseproof paper, then brush each with melted butter. Spoon the meringue mixture evenly between each tin and bake in a pre-heated oven at 325°F, 160°C, Gas mark 3 for 40 minutes. Turn out onto a cooling tray, carefully peel off the greaseproof paper and leave until cold.

To make the chocolate filling, cream the butter and icing sugar together before adding the melted chocolate. Whip the double cream in a separate bowl and keep three tablespoonfuls aside in a smaller bowl for decoration. Wash and hull the strawberries, keep half for decoration and roughly chop the remaining half. Combine these with the whipped cream.

Place one meringue on a serving plate. Cover with half of the chocolate filling, then half of the strawberry cream filling. Place a second meringue on top and spread this with the remaining chocolate and strawberry cream before finishing with the final meringue. Decorate the meringue with the reserved cream and strawberries. This is best served straight from the fridge.

Great-Aunt Isa's Iced Sponge

My mum and aunt fondly recall this recipe made by their Aunt Isa which she passed to my granny. The cream needs to be very stiffly whipped to hold the weight of the icing.

Ingredients:

4oz/115g softened butter

4oz/115g caster sugar

2 eggs, lightly beaten

4oz/115g self-raising flour, sifted

½pt/280ml double cream

8oz/225g icing sugar

2 tbsp water

Preparation:

Grease and lightly flour a baking tray. Cream the butter and caster sugar until fluffy and slowly beat in the eggs. Add the flour and fold into the mixture using a metal spoon. Pour the mixture into the baking tray and smooth over the surface. Bake in a pre-heated oven at 350°F, 180°C, Gas mark 4 for approximately 15 minutes until the sponge is springy to the touch. Turn out and cool on a wire cooling tray.

Whip the cream until very stiff and spoon this onto the sponge. Mix the icing sugar with the water to a thin, runny consistency and pour immediately over the cream. Cover with hundreds and thousands or chocolate flakes and leave to set before cutting into squares.

CHAPTER 2

Dead Flies

———◆———

Hunger wid break through stane wa's.
Hunger can drive people to desperation.

Scots saying[7]

{ In this chapter, I've chosen food that I absolutely
hated as a child – the stuff kids usually loathe but
we're told that we'll have better eyesight, curlier
hair, etc, if we *sup it up* like good wee *weans*.
Some I have grown to love, some I've tried to
cook another way to make them more appealing,
and some – well, let's just say that there are some
tastes that are best avoided! }

Vegetable Broth (serves 6)

As a child, I used to call this 'Dead Fly Soup'. I refused to eat it because I was convinced that the tiny dark green 'bits' of the vegetable leaves were dead flies floating in the bowl!

Ingredients:

½ teacup barley

1 teacup red lentils

2 white onions, sliced

2 leeks, sliced

2 sticks of celery, sliced

2 large carrots, sliced

3pts/1.7L vegetable or chicken stock

Parsley, chopped

Salt and pepper

Preparation:

When I know I'm going to be making soup, I keep the water left over from any vegetables boiled the day before and use this as my base stock.

To make a chicken stock, put the carcass and remaining scraps into a large saucepan, add water until about ¾ of it is covered, season and bring to the boil, then simmer for about an hour and leave overnight. Everyone has their own way of making stock – the main thing is to produce a flavour that enhances the soup. We add boiled potatoes if having this for a main meal.

Put barley and lentils into a large saucepan, add the stock and bring to the boil. Add vegetables, stir well and reduce heat until simmering. Season, add half of the chopped parsley, cover with lid and cook for 1 hour. Add remainder of parsley just before serving.

Scotch Broth

This is a hearty Scottish soup traditionally made with mutton but nowadays lamb is more often used. As a child, I hated the amount of barley used in the broth but this is a recipe which has grown on me – probably because it is 'comfort food' when the weather is bitter outside.

Ingredients:

3lb/1.35kg neck of lamb (or mutton)

½ cup pearl barley

2 tbsp butter

1 large onion, chopped

3 carrots, diced

1 small turnip, diced

3 sticks celery, chopped

Seasoning

Preparation:

Place the lamb in a large saucepan and cover with cold water. Bring to the boil, add the barley, cover and simmer for approximately 2 hours until the meat and barley are tender. Add more water to allow for any that has boiled off. Skim the soup to remove any surface fat. Remove the meat from the soup and cut into small pieces, throwing away the bones. Return the meat to the soup and continue to simmer.

Melt the butter in a frying pan, add the vegetables and cook for 10 minutes until softened. Add the vegetables to the soup and simmer for a further 15 minutes. Season to taste.

Cullen Skink

I hated fish and the thought of eating it in a soup abhorred me – until I tasted the American 'chowder'. Cullen Skink is a thick, creamy Scottish fish soup similar to the 'chowder'. Cullen is a small fishing village in Moray, on the North East coast of Scotland. *Skink* was an old Scots word originally referring to the shin or hough of beef, but was later translated as 'a thick soup'.

Ingredients:

2lb/900g smoked haddock

1 medium onion, finely chopped

1½ pt/900ml milk

8oz/225g cooked potato, roughly chopped

1 bay leaf

Seasoning

Parsley, finely chopped

2 tbsp butter

Preparation:

Place the fish in a shallow pan and cover with water, skin side down. Bring to the boil and simmer for 5 minutes. Take the fish out and remove the skin and bones. Flake the fish and return to the pan. Add the onion, bay leaf and seasoning, and simmer for another 10 minutes. Strain off the stock, remove the bay leaf and place the fish aside, keeping it warm. Return the strained stock to the pan, add the milk and bring to the boil. Add the cooked potato chunks and the flaked fish. Check the seasoning and add more if necessary.

Serve in bowls with dots of butter on top (which melt through the soup) and chopped parsley sprinkled over. Triangles of buttered toast can be served alongside.

Beetroot Soup with Soured Cream

I used to take beetroot sandwiches to school – yes, honestly. By the time it came to lunchtime, the sarnies were bright pink and limp but for some unknown reason, I loved these. Then, it was the texture of the beetroot slipping over the butter in my mouth on the way down that I found extremely gratifying. Now, I would be struggling not to have it slipping back up.

Here's a beetroot recipe – bread optional – that I devised whilst attending a course 'Menu Planning Using Local Produce' in Falkirk College, Scotland.

Ingredients:

1lb/450g raw beetroot, finely chopped

1 medium onion, finely chopped

1 celery stick, finely chopped

2 medium carrots, grated

2 pts/1.1L beef stock

Bay leaf

Salt and pepper

1 small carton soured cream

Preparation:

Put the beetroot, onion, carrots, celery, stock and bay leaf into a large saucepan and bring to the boil. Reduce heat, add seasoning to taste, cover and simmer for approximately 1 hour. Use a hand blender or food processor to blend the ingredients together. Taste and adjust seasoning if necessary. Serve in bowls with a spoonful of soured cream in the centre.

Cream of Cauliflower, Bacon and Sorrel Soup

I love cauliflower cheese but the thought of cauliflower in a soup did not appeal until I made this recipe in which the creaminess of the cauliflower is complemented by salty bacon and the tangy bite of sorrel, a green leafy vegetable (or herb) similar to spinach.

*A word of warning though – sorrel contains oxalic acid, therefore it can be poisonous if eaten in large quantities but is harmless in smaller quantities.

Ingredients:

2 tbsp oil

1 medium onion, chopped

8 rashers of Ulster smoked back bacon, cut into strips

2 medium cauliflowers, chopped into florets

1 stick of celery, sliced

1 small leek, sliced

2 pt/1.1L vegetable stock

Seasoning

6 sorrel leaves, shredded

Preparation:

Heat the oil in a large saucepan and add the chopped onions and bacon strips. Cook for 2 minutes stirring occasionally. Remove the bacon and set aside. Add the cauliflower, celery and leeks, and cook for a further 5 minutes. Stir in the stock and half of the sorrel. Season to taste (be aware of the saltiness of the bacon), bring to the boil and simmer for 15 minutes. Add the remainder of the bacon and simmer for a further 5 minutes. Liquidise in a food processor or use a hand blender. Add the cream, heat through and garnish with the remaining sorrel leaves.

Suppin' loud's nae company.
Don't slurp when supping soup.

Scots Saying[8]

Root and Cider Hotpot

Turnip is my most hated food of all time. When I was a *wean*, my granny would have served this up with boiled potatoes, fried bacon, and sometimes put cubes of bread through the mashed turnip. Of course, the bread swelled and softened, the idea being to make the dinner go that bit further but it was enough to put me off! I've therefore struggled to find a recipe that brings out the good side of turnip, and decided that it's best served mingled with other flavours, as in this hotpot!

Ingredients:

8oz/225g turnips

8oz/225g carrots

8oz/225g parsnips

2 onions, sliced

2 leeks, sliced

1lb/450g potatoes, peeled and very thinly sliced

3oz/85g butter

1½oz/45g plain flour

1 tbsp tomato puree

1 tsp Worcester sauce

¾ pint/425ml dry cider

Salt and pepper

Oil for brushing

3oz/85g Ulster Cheddar, grated

Preparation:

Cut turnip, carrots and parsnips into chunks and add to melted butter in a frying pan with the onions and leeks. Cook gently until softened and transfer to a large casserole dish. Mix the flour with a little of the cider in the pan and stir in the remaining cider. Bring mixture to the boil, stirring until it becomes a thick sauce. Add puree, seasoning and Worcester sauce, and pour over the vegetables in the casserole dish. Place the thin slices of potato over the top, brush with the oil and scatter over the cheese.

Cover with casserole lid or foil and bake in a pre-heated oven at 400°F, 200°C, Gas mark 6 for approximately 1½ hours or until the vegetables are cooked through. Uncover the dish, and cook for a further 15–20 minutes or until the topping is golden brown.

Jeff's Lamb Stew

Stew is a great favourite in Ulster and is enjoyed in both cold and warm weather! My mum makes a big pot of stew using either beef, lamb, chicken, or even corned beef to create a variety of flavours. When I had my cafés, I would regularly have included some kind of stew on the menu.

My brother's forte (apart from serving up a mean Ulster Fry) is lamb stew. He's inherited our late father's passion for motorcycle road racing (one of Ulster's top sports) and follows the Ulster Grand Prix circuit through the year. He likes nothing better than to come home to a big bowl of stew after a cold, wet day watching the races. This is his simple recipe, adapted from my mother's original one, and one which even I will eat, having hated stew as a child.

Ingredients:

2lb/900g neck of lamb

Water

Seasoning

2 large onions, sliced

4 large carrots, sliced

6 medium potatoes, sliced

Preparation:

Place the lamb in a large saucepan, season and cover with cold water (about 1½inch/3.8cm) from the bottom of the pan. Bring to the boil and simmer slowly for 1¼–1½ hours.

Lift the lamb from the saucepan and set aside. Put the onions and carrots in the saucepan and simmer for 5 minutes before adding the potatoes. Season again and simmer for 25 minutes, stirring frequently to prevent the vegetables sticking to the bottom.

While the vegetables are stewing, pull the meat from the bone. When the vegetables are soft, add the meat and warm through. Adjust the seasoning if necessary and serve in bowls with crusty, wheaten or soda bread.

Liver and Bacon Casserole

The next two recipes use liver and kidneys which I hated as a child but now love. Lamb's liver is not as strong as that of a pig or calf, so I've used it in the first recipe.

Ingredients:

1lb/450g lamb's liver

8oz/225g unsmoked back bacon

2 onions

2 tbsp plain flour

1 tsp powdered mustard

8 fl oz/230ml water

3 tbsp sherry

Salt and black pepper

Bay leaf

Parsley

Oil for frying

Preparation:

Trim liver and cut into slices. Mix flour, mustard, salt and pepper, and dip liver slices into this, coating both sides. Cut bacon into small pieces and fry in a little oil. Remove from pan and place in bottom of a large casserole dish. Slice onions and fry in oil until soft. Place on top of bacon. Fry liver slices on both sides until golden, then place on top of onions. Add any remaining seasoned flour to the pan and stir in water and sherry. Cook until thickened, then pour into the casserole dish. Add bay leaf and cook in a pre-heated oven at 350°F, 180°C, Gas mark 4 for 35 minutes. Just before serving, remove the bay leaf and add chopped parsley to the casserole.

Kidney and Mushroom Casserole

Sherry and mushrooms are a classic combination.

Ingredients:

1lb/450g kidneys, skinned and chopped

4oz/115g onions, chopped

8oz/225g mushrooms, quartered

½ pint/280ml beef stock

4 fl oz/115ml sherry

5oz/140g soured cream

Seasoning

Preparation:

Cook kidneys under a hot grill for 1 minute each side. Place in casserole dish and add onions, stock, sherry, mushrooms and seasoning. Cover and bake in a pre-heated oven at 400°F, 200°C, Gas mark 6 for approximately 40 minutes. Just before serving, stir in soured cream.

Chicken and Leek Crumble

Leeks are in season almost all year round and broad beans are plentiful from late spring to mid autumn. The leaves of the herb lovage, have a similar taste to celery. Leeks and broad beans were the sort of vegetables I didn't like as a child because leeks seemed too slimy and broad beans seemed too hard. The recipe envelopes the vegetables in a creamy, cheesy sauce to bring out the flavour whilst an oaty topping gives this savoury crumble a bit of a 'crunch!'

Ingredients:

1oz/30g butter

1oz/30g plain flour

¾ pt/425ml milk

Seasoning

4 large chicken breast fillets, cooked and sliced

2 large leeks, sliced

6oz/170g broad beans, cooked and drained

2 tsp lovage leaves, shredded

2oz/55g Ballybrie soft cheese, roughly sliced

Topping:
3oz/85g butter

6oz/170g plain flour

2oz/55g porridge oats

1 tsp mustard powder

Preparation:

Put the broad beans in a small saucepan of salted water and bring to the boil. Simmer for 5 minutes, then drain and set aside.

Melt the butter in a large saucepan, stir in the flour and cook for 1 minute. Slowly add the milk and stir until the sauce thickens. Season to taste, add the lovage, leeks, beans and chicken and simmer for 10 minutes. Add the cheese, stirring until it melts through the sauce, then spoon the mixture into an ovenproof dish.

To make the crumble topping, rub the butter into the flour and stir in the oats and mustard powder. Sprinkle this over the chicken and leek mixture and bake in a pre-heated oven at 400°F, 200°C, Gas mark 6 for 20–25 minutes.

Big Fish with Mealacrochie Crust

Mealacrochie or Mealie Crushie (depending on where you come from) is an Ulster-Scots recipe for oatmeal fried in hot bacon fat with onions. Sounds grim but is actually very tasty! Ling is a deep water fish found in the North Sea off the coast of Northern Ireland. If ling is unavailable, use cod instead.

Ingredients:

4 Ling fillets

2 tbsp olive oil

4oz/115g breadcrumbs

2 tbsp oatmeal

1 small onion, finely chopped

1 tbsp basil, finely chopped

1 tbsp rosemary, chopped

1 tbsp parsley, finely chopped

Salt and freshly ground black pepper

4 tbsp bacon fat

Preparation:

Dip the ling in the olive oil. Mix the breadcrumbs and oatmeal with the onion and herbs, then season. Coat both sides of each fillet in the mixture. Melt the bacon fat in a large griddle or frying pan and cook each side until crisp, then reduce the heat to allow the fish to cook through for about 5–8 minutes.

Creamy Rice Pudding with Blackberry Compote

Rice pudding reminds most people of school dinners but this recipe reminds me of Sunday dinner in granny and grandpas' house after church. I never saw my grandmother use a cookbook – most recipes were passed down from mother to daughter. Granny would make her rice pudding in a saucepan on the stove or bake it in the oven until a brown skin was formed. A dollop of soft fruit compote in the centre gave a wonderful sweetness to balance the creaminess of the pudding.

Ingredients:

2oz/55g pudding rice

1 pt/570ml milk

3 tbsp caster sugar

Few drops of vanilla essence

Small tub of double cream

Blackberry

Compote:

8oz/225g blackberries

4oz/115g caster sugar

1 tsp lemon rind

1 tbsp blackberry jam

Preparation:

Put the rice, milk, sugar and vanilla into a large saucepan and bring to the boil, stirring until the sugar has dissolved. Reduce heat and simmer for approximately 45 minutes, but remember to stir every 5 to 10 minutes or the rice will stick to the bottom and burn. If the pudding becomes too thick, add more milk. When cooked, pour the rice into a bowl and allow to cool down.

Whip the cream and add to the cooled rice. Wash the berries and put into a pan with the sugar, rind and jam. Cook over a low heating stirring continuously until the fruit is soft. Pour into a bowl and leave to chill.

Lemon Suet Pudding

As a child, I ate some unusual sandwich fillings – sugar sarnies and suet sarnies were favourites! The suet sandwich memory comes from standing in my granny's scullery waiting impatiently while she cut the warm suet (fat) off the Sunday roast, parcelled it in a slice of white unbuttered plain bread, and passed it to me. It tasted heavenly then – not so sure about suet now! Here's a recipe – improvised from a school cookery class – for an old-fashioned suet pudding, the type we used to have after a Sunday dinner. The 'cup' I use is just an ordinary teacup.

Ingredients:

1 cup suet, shredded

3 cups plain flour, sifted

1 tsp baking soda

1 tsp cinnamon

½ tsp nutmeg

1 tsp lemon rind

1 cup sultanas

1 tsp salt

1 cup milk

1 cup golden syrup

Preparation:

Grease individual pudding moulds or one pudding basin. Mix all the dry ingredients with the fruit in a large bowl. Make a well in the centre and gradually stir in the milk and syrup until the mixture is well blended. Pour into pudding moulds or basin, cover with greaseproof paper and then with kitchen foil. Tie firmly, then put the bowls into a large pan with water coming halfway up the sides, cover with lid and steam for 3 hours. Check every so often that the water does not boil away and add more water if necessary. Serve hot with custard or pouring cream.

Auntie's Bran Loaf

Another food I hate is bran, which we've been told is extremely good for us. The stick things that pass for cereal have appeared on many diets I've tried over the years and I've never been able to get past the first mouthful – until my Aunt Anthea gave me this recipe. Eat up and feel holier than thou!

Ingredients:

1 cup All Bran

1 cup soft brown sugar

1 cup milk

1 cup dried fruit (e.g. sultanas and raisins)

1 cup desiccated coconut

1 cup mixed nuts (e.g. walnuts, pecan)

1 cup self-raising flour

Preparation:

Place all ingredients – except for the flour – in a large bowl and steep for 1 hour. Add the flour and mix well. Pour into a greased, lined loaf tin and bake in a pre-heated oven at 350°F, 180°C, Gas mark 4 for approximately 1¼ to 1½ hours. To make sure the loaf is cooked the whole way through, insert a skewer into the centre and if the skewer comes out 'clean', it's cooked.

Annie Bell's Paneada

Paneada is a recipe my great-grandmother used to make when one of her granddaughters was poorly. She would boil some milk and soak slices of bread in it until the bread was sodden having absorbed all the milk. Apparently they weren't that keen on it, so I've added it to my 'Dead Fly' list. It can also be made with cheese – as in this recipe – but during the war cheese was rationed and therefore considered a luxury.

Ingredients:

4 slices bread, preferably plain loaf

2 cups milk

2 eggs

2 tbsp butter

2 cups grated cheese

Salt and pepper

Preparation:

Layer bread with the cheese in a greased ovenproof dish and season well. Boil the milk and leave to cool. Beat the eggs and add to the milk. Pour over the bread, dot with the butter and bake in a pre-heated oven at 400°F, 200°C, Gas mark 6 for approximately 20–25 minutes or until golden.

Now rich sweetmilk and buttered bread
Were handed round the boone.

Henry McDonald Flecher, Bard of Ballinderry (1827–?)[9]

Parritch

Parritch – the Ulster-Scots for 'porridge' – is traditionally a thin oatmeal. We were encouraged to eat porridge in the winter before setting off for school to set us up for the cold day ahead, but we hated it. It wasn't until later years that I began to get a liking for this hearty breakfast and as it's reported to help lower cholesterol, it seems to be back in fashion.

Nowadays, porridge is easier to make in the microwave but this recipe makes it the old-fashioned way, the way I was taught when I worked in a Scottish hotel! Remember to stir the porridge in a clockwise direction – myth has it that if you stir anti-clockwise, tha *De'il wull nab ye!*

Ingredients:

2 heaped tbsp oatmeal

1pt/570ml milk

½ cup boiling water

1 tbsp Mourne Heather Honey

1 tbsp raisins

Preparation:

Put the oatmeal into a bowl, add the milk and stir well. Add the water and stir again.

Leave to stand for 1 hour, stirring occasionally. Drain the mixture into a saucepan, bring almost to the boil stirring consistently, reduce heat and simmer for approximately 10 minutes. Mix the honey and raisins through the parritch and serve.

Stoke up wi' the porridge.
Without a hearty start to the day, you'll soon tire.

Scots Saying[10]

CHAPTER 3

A Family Gaitherin

———◆———

I loll'd upon a cushion'd chair,
An' fed on rich an' dainty fare.

Hugh Porter, Bard of Moneyslane (1781–?)[11]

{ July and September are our busiest months in
the family, with a wedding anniversary and
seven birthdays. We tend to have one big family
gaitherin to cover everything and I usually do all
the catering myself. The only thing I hate about
entertaining is the final half hour before everyone
is due and the last minute rush is on to ensure
everything is cooked, hot and edible! Here are
some of my favourite recipes tried and tested on
kith an' kin. }

Ballyblue, Apricot and Honey Stuffed Pears

I made this as a starter to a family celebration meal and it went down a treat. The combination of sweet pear and honey with the creaminess of the blue cheese is wonderful. The stuffing can be made in advance but prepare the pears just before serving to prevent them from colouring.

Ingredients:

4 large fresh pears

4 tbsp Ballyblue soft cheese

2 tbsp soured cream

6 dried apricots, soaked in hot water

4 tbsp Mourne Heather Honey

1 tbsp chopped walnuts

Leaves for garnish (e.g. curly endive, watercress)

Preparation:

Soak the apricots in hot water for at least 30 minutes until soft enough to chop finely. In a bowl, mix the apricots with the cheese and the soured cream until well combined. Wash and peel the pears, slice in half and remove the core, allowing one pear per person. Place two halves on each plate and garnish with the lettuce. Stuff the centre of each half with the cheese mixture, drizzle the honey over the pears, and sprinkle with the walnuts.

Salmon Chowder

Mainly due to poverty, famine and religious persecution, the eighteenth century saw almost 250,000 Ulster-Scots set sail from Ulster to start a new life in the 'New World', many emigrating to Canada. This recipe was given to me by a Canadian family friend, Betty Wilson, who is originally from Northern Ireland.

Ingredients:

4 small salmon fillets, cooked and flaked (or 2 small tins of salmon, drained)

2 medium potatoes, cubed

1 carrot, cubed

½ cup celery, sliced

1 medium onion, chopped

2 cups water

1½ tsp salt

3 tbsp butter

4 tbsp plain flour

2 cups milk

½ tsp Worcester sauce

Preparation:

Mix the water and salt and bring to the boil in a saucepan. Add the potatoes and carrot and cook for 10 minutes. Drain and reserve the water. Add the butter to a separate pan and fry the onion until soft. Stir in the flour and milk and cook until thickened. Add the cooked vegetables, reserved liquid, celery, salmon and Worcester sauce. Heat through and serve.

Chicken and Dressing Casserole (serves 6)

This is a recipe given to me by Joyce, another Canadian friend, and it's a useful one for using up leftover chicken and stuffing (or dressing, as it's called in Canada).

Ingredients:

8 chicken breasts

Oil or butter for frying

1 large onion, chopped

2 cups Oakwood Cheddar, grated

2 tins condensed cream of chicken (or mushroom) soup

Stuffing:

2 cups breadcrumbs

1 cup finely chopped onion

1 tbsp finely chopped parsley

1 tbsp butter, melted

Seasoning

Preparation:

Cut chicken into pieces and brown in a frying pan with a little oil or butter. Add the onion to the pan and cook until it softens. Layer the chicken, soup, onions and cheese – in this order – in a deep casserole dish. Make the stuffing by mixing the ingredients together and placing on top of the cheese. Cover the dish with a lid or foil and bake in a pre-heated oven at 350°F, 180°C, Gas mark 4 for 1 hour. Remove the lid or foil and bake for a further 10 minutes.

Virginia Baked Ham with Pear Chutney

During the eighteenth century, almost 250,000 Ulster-Scots emigrants – mostly Scottish Presbyterians – settled in North East America, in Pennsylvania, Maryland, Massachusetts, New Hampshire, New York, and New Jersey. Later settlements moved to South East America and the Appalachian Mountains area, arriving in North and South Carolina, Virginia, Kentucky, Tennessee, Alabama and Georgia.

The Virginia-style ham was created by colonists in the town of Smithfield, in the Isle of Wight County of Virginia. They dry cured the meat in salt, smoked it slowly then aged it for several months, the end result being smokier and saltier than most 'Old World' hams. This recipe is a shorter version.

Ingredients:

10lb/4.5kg dry-cured, smoked ham

3 tbsp soft brown sugar

2 tsp freshly cracked black pepper

1 cup whiskey

Pear chutney:

1½lb pears, peeled, cored and chopped

1½ cups soft brown sugar

1½ cups cider vinegar

1 cup raisins

1 cup onion, chopped finely

1 rind of a lemon

½ tsp cayenne pepper

Pinch ground cinnamon

Pinch ground ginger

Pinch ground cloves

Preparation:

Wash the ham and cover with water. Soak for 24 hours, changing the water often. Place the ham, skin side down, in a large saucepan with enough fresh water to cover it. Simmer for 20–25 minutes per pound.

Place the ham in a roasting pan, make diagonal scores in the skin, pour over the whiskey and sprinkle on the sugar and pepper. Bake in a pre-heated oven at 375°F, 190°C, Gas mark 5 for 30–40 minutes or until the ham is glazed. Set aside to rest at room temperature for about 20 minutes before thinly slicing.

To make the chutney, put the pears in a saucepan and just cover them with water. Bring to the boil and simmer until the pears become slightly soft – do not overcook. Pour off the cooking liquid into a small heavy saucepan and mix in the sugar. Bring to the boil and reduce the mixture down to a syrup, approximately 10–15 minutes. Stir the remaining ingredients into the pears and add the syrup. Bring to the boil and simmer for 45 minutes or until the chutney has thickened. Drain off any excess liquid. Leave to cool and serve with the ham.

Appalachian Chicken

Each Southern American State has its own version of Southern Fried Chicken. This recipe is a version from the Appalachian Mountain region, an area stretching from Pennsylvania (and parts of New York State) in the North to Alabama in the South. It is the area to which most Ulster-Scots emigrants flocked in the eighteenth century and later inspired the famous Bluegrass music tradition.

Ingredients:

4 cups oil

4 chicken breasts

4 cups plain flour

2 eggs, beaten

1½ cups buttermilk

¾ cup water

4 tsp salt

Appalachian

Seasoning:

2 tbsp dark brown sugar

1 tsp garlic salt

1 tbsp dried oregano

1 tsp ground chilli flakes

1 tbsp paprika

Preparation:

Mix all ingredients for the seasoning together in a bowl.

Wipe the chicken breasts dry with paper towels. Put 2 cups of the flour onto a large flat plate and dip the breasts into it, on both sides. Shake off excess flour and leave to the side.

In a shallow dish, mix the beaten eggs, water and buttermilk. On a large plate, mix the Appalachian seasoning with the remaining 2 cups of flour and the salt.

Dip the chicken breasts in the buttermilk mixture, then in the seasoning mixture, shaking off any excess flour. Heat the oil in a large pan until hot – drop a cube of bread into the oil and if it browns quickly, the oil is hot enough. Fry each chicken breast until it is golden brown taking care not to overcrowd the pan or the chicken will not cook through, approximately 5–8 minutes. Put the chicken in a roasting pan and bake in a pre-heated oven at 375°F, 190°C, Gas mark 5 for 30–40 minutes.

Stuffed Pork Fillet with Apricot, Onion and Parsley Stuffing

This is a favourite Sunday roast in our house. Like the traditional apple accompaniment, the apricot stuffing lifts the flavour of the pork.

Ingredients:

1 large pork fillet

6oz/170g breadcrumbs

1½oz/45g no-soak dried apricots, finely chopped

1 small onion, finely chopped

1 oz/30g butter

1 small egg, beaten

Seasoning

1 tbsp fresh parsley, finely chopped

Preparation:

Fry the onion and apricots in the butter until softened. Add the breadcrumbs, parsley, egg and seasoning and stir until evenly combined – the mixture should be slightly 'sticky' so that it binds together.

Spread the pork fillet on a chopping board and lightly score the surface – be careful not to cut through the flesh – and gently ease out the fillet ready for the stuffing. Pack the stuffing onto the fillet and roll up from one end, careful not to cram too much stuffing into the roll otherwise it will spill out during cooking. You can either tie the fillet with string or, as I prefer, use metal skewers to hold the fillet together. Place on a greased roasting dish, dot with butter and season. Cook in a pre-heated oven at 375°F, 190°C, Gas mark 5 for approximately 1 hour. Serve with potatoes and vegetables.

Cidered Pork

County Armagh is famous for its Bramley apples, cider and apple juice, and nothing tastes better with pork than apples.

Ingredients:

1lb/450g Ulster pork fillet, cut into strips

1 large onion, sliced

2oz/55g butter

2oz/55g plain flour

½pt/280ml traditional (Armagh) cider

4oz/115g mushrooms, sliced

Seasoning

¼pt/140ml double cream

Paprika

Preparation:

Sauté the onion and pork in the butter for 5 minutes. Stir in the flour and gradually add the cider. Cover and simmer for approximately 20 minutes. Add the mushrooms and cook for a further 5 minutes. Season to taste and stir in the cream. Serve with boiled rice and sprinkle with paprika.

An in the wicked whup an flail o
Brenches, the batterin o
Shoorin epples an juntherin thud
O grun at last.

James Fenton, contemporary Ulster-Scots poet[12]

Patrick's Bacon and Pamphrey Pie (serves 6)

In Northern Ireland, 17 March is the day we Ulster-Scots celebrate the life of Patrick, the Apostle of Ulster. Patrick was born towards the end of the fourth century, the son of a British churchman, and performed most of his missionary work in Ulster where he was converted, where he preached, where he died and was buried – and where he did not drive snakes out of Ireland despite the common myth!

Ingredients:

12 bacon chops

2 medium pamphrey (dark green, leafy spring cabbage)

4oz/115g butter

2 Bramley apples (peeled, cored and quartered)

1 large red onion, sliced

2 cloves garlic, crushed

¼ tsp grated nutmeg

Seasoning

Grated rind of an orange

4oz/115g soft brown sugar

¾ pt/425ml red wine

2 tbsp red wine vinegar

4 tbsp water

Preparation:

Wash the pamphrey, discarding the stalk and outer leaves, and shred finely. Melt the butter in a large pan and fry the pamphrey until softened (10 minutes). Layer a casserole dish with half of the cabbage and its juice, and half of the onions, apples, garlic, nutmeg, rind and seasoning. Repeat with the remainder. Sprinkle over the sugar, and add the water, wine and vinegar. Cover and cook in a pre-heated oven at 375°F, 190°C, Gas mark 5 for 45 minutes. Grill the bacon chops for 2 minutes on each side until browned, then arrange on top of the casserole and cook, uncovered, for 30 –35 minutes. Serve with champ.

Kilkeel Fisherman's Pie (serves 6)

Kilkeel is the capital of an ancient area in County Down known as 'The Kingdom of Mourne' and has a large Ulster-Scots community. Kilkeel meaning 'the church of the narrows' takes its name from thirteenth century church ruins in the centre of the town. It is set amongst the beautiful Mourne Mountains and surrounded by the Irish Sea. Its main occupations are fishing and farming, and it currently has the largest fishing fleet in Northern Ireland.

Ingredients:

14oz/400g cod

8oz/225g peeled, cooked prawns

Seasoning

Large knob of butter

2oz/55g plain flour

2oz/55g butter

1pt/570ml milk

Seasoning

4 hard boiled eggs, halved

1 small can sweetcorn, drained

6oz/170g Ulster Cheddar Cheese, grated

½ tsp mild curry powder

1 tbsp parsley, chopped finely

2lb/900g potato, seasoned and mashed with butter and cream

Preparation:

Season the cod, dot with butter and fry, skin side down, in a frying pan for about 8 minutes or until fish flakes easily. Place in the bottom of an ovenproof dish and leave to cool, then cover with the prawns and eggs.

Make the white sauce by melting the butter in a saucepan and adding the flour. Stir over a medium heat for 1 minute until the flour is cooked. Gradually add the milk, stirring continuously over a medium heat until the milk is blended and the sauce begins to thicken. Season to taste and add the sweetcorn, parsley, curry powder and half of the cheese.

Pour over the fish. Cover with the mashed potato and remaining cheese. Bake in a pre-heated oven at 400°F, 200°C, Gas mark 6 for 20–25 minutes until golden. Serve with a green salad.

Salmon Fishcakes with Lemon Sauce

Fishcakes are so easy to make using left over potato to bind the flakes of fish together. Although most fish will work in this dish, I tried this recipe using salmon and a fresh lemon sauce which is a perfect accompaniment to fish in general.

Ingredients:

12oz/340g salmon fillets, cooked

1lb/450g mashed potato, cold

1 tbsp parsley, finely chopped

1oz/30g butter

2 tbsp double cream

1 tsp Worcester sauce

Seasoning

Butter and oil for frying

Flour for dusting

Lemon Sauce:

3 tbsp fresh lemon juice

1oz/30g unsalted butter

¼ pt/140ml double cream

Preparation:

Flake the cooked salmon and mash in a large bowl with the potatoes, parsley, butter, cream, Worcester sauce, and season to taste. Shape into rounds and dust both sides with flour. Cover with cling film and put in the fridge for about an hour to stiffen. Melt the butter and oil in a frying pan, and fry for about 5 minutes each side until golden. Remove and place in a heatproof dish, and bake in a pre-heated oven at 400°F, 200°C, Gas mark 6 for 10–15 minutes.

To make the lemon sauce, melt the butter in the pan and add the cream. Heat through, then add the lemon juice but do not let the sauce boil or it will curdle. Season and pour over the fishcakes. Serve with champ or a side salad.

Country Lamb

Frozen peas are every bit as nutritious as fresh, and the combination of lamb, peas and mint is a classic combination.

Ingredients:

1½lb/680g lamb steaks

2 tbsp flour seasoned with salt and black pepper

2oz/55g butter

14oz/400g can plum tomatoes

4oz/115g garden peas

Fresh mint

Seasoning

Preparation:

Drain tomatoes and reserve juice. Cube steaks and toss in seasoned flour, shaking off the excess. Melt butter in large pan, add lamb cubes and cook until browned. Add drained tomatoes with 4 tbsp of the reserved juice. Cover, reduce heat and simmer for ¾ hour before adding the peas. Cook for a further 5 minutes or until the lamb is cooked. Add freshly chopped mint and season to taste. Serve with champ.

Carrot and Pineapple Cake with Cream Cheese Icing

This is the way I like my carrot cake – moist with a sweet, creamy topping. Pineapple is obviously not a local ingredient but its addition to the carrots is what keeps this cake moist. I use a teacup for measuring the ingredients.

Ingredients:

2 cups plain flour

2 tsp baking powder

2 cups caster sugar

1½ cups grated carrots

1 cup sultanas

1½ cups sunflower oil

8oz/225g tin crushed pineapple

4 eggs

1 tsp cinnamon

2 tsp vanilla essence

Icing:

1lb/450g icing sugar

8oz/225g cream cheese

Preparation:

Mix all ingredients together in a large bowl. Pour into 3 lined and greased 8inch/20.5cm tins. Bake in a pre-heated oven at 350°F, 180°C, Gas mark 4 for approximately 30 minutes or until the cake springs back when lightly pressed. Remove from the tins and cool.

To make the icing, mix the sugar and cream cheese together. Sandwich the layers together with half of the icing before covering the top with the remainder.

The salt sea we'll harry, and bring to our Charlie
The cream from the bothy and curd from the pen.

James Hogg, Scottish poet (1770–1835)[13]

Rhubarb and Oat Crumble (serves 6)

We used to have rhubarb growing in our back garden which was very useful when it came to Sunday pudding. Porridge oats added to a traditional crumble mix gives a nice crunch to this dessert in contrast with the softness of the cooked rhubarb.

Ingredients:

8oz/225g rhubarb

4oz/115g soft brown sugar

Rind of an orange, finely grated

3oz/85g plain flour

3oz/85g Scotch porridge oats

3oz/85g soft brown sugar

3oz/85g butter, softened

Preparation:

Wash and slice the rhubarb and place in a buttered pie dish. Sprinkle over 4oz/115g of the sugar with the rind. Rub the butter into the flour, add the 3oz/85g of the sugar and the porridge oats. Mix well and spread over the rhubarb. Bake in a pre-heated oven at 350°F, 180°C or Gas mark 4 for 35–40 minutes or until topping is golden. Serve with custard, or locally-made ice cream.

Apple and Raspberry Tart

My grandmother made a special apple tart for Hallowe'en with a sixpence and a thrupenny bit hidden in the filling, wrapped in greaseproof paper. Everyone tucked in with great care, until the lucky person located the 'treasure!'

Ingredients:

8oz/225g shortcrust pastry

2oz/55g caster sugar

4 large Bramley apples

2oz/55g fresh Scottish raspberries

Pinch cinnamon

Pinch nutmeg

Preparation:

Cut pastry into two batches. Roll out one batch on a lightly floured surface and use to line a greased pie plate. Put in a fridge to rest.

Wash, peel and core the apples, cut into thick chunks and cook on top of the stove with the sugar and a little water. When soft, drain the excess liquid, add the spices, and leave to cool. Add the raspberries to the cooked apple mixture, taking care not to break the raspberries when stirring. Remove the plate from the fridge and spoon the fruit onto the pastry.

Roll out the second batch of pastry. Brush the edges with cold water then cover the fruit with the pastry lid. Trim the excess. Using a fork (or your fingers), press the edges of the two pastry rounds together, then prick the pastry lid all over. Bake in a pre-heated oven at 375°F, 190°C, Gas mark 5 for approximately 30 minutes until golden. Dust with caster sugar while still hot and serve with custard, or locally-made ice cream.

Rhubarb Meringue Pie

Another good use for the rhubarb growing wild in our back garden! This recipe is a change from the traditional Lemon Meringue Pie.

Ingredients:

8oz/225g shortcrust pastry

1lb/450g rhubarb

7oz/200g caster sugar

2 oranges (grated rind and juice)

1oz/30g cornflour

2 egg yolks

Meringue:

2 egg whites

4oz/115g caster sugar

Preparation:

Roll out the pastry to line a greased pie dish and prick the pastry all over. Bake blind by covering the base with greaseproof paper and filling the centre with uncooked rice or dried peas. Bake in a pre-heated oven at 400°F, 200°C or Gas mark 6 for 15 minutes.

Wash and chop the rhubarb into cubes. Place in a large saucepan and add 4oz/115g of the caster sugar and the orange peel. Simmer over a low heat until cooked, strain the juice into a separate bowl, and set the rhubarb aside to cool. Mix the cornflour with the orange juice, egg yolks, the remaining 3oz/85g of caster sugar, and the reserved rhubarb juice in a saucepan over a low heat until the mixture thickens and a custard is formed. Add the cooled rhubarb to the pastry dish and cover with the custard.

Beat the egg whites until stiff, then fold in the 4oz/115g caster sugar. Pile high on top of the custard and return to a cooler oven (350°F, 180°C, Gas mark 4) for approximately 15 minutes or until the meringue is golden.

Butterscotch Pudding

When working in a hotel in Scotland over the Christmas holiday, the manager gave me a collection of old and new Scottish recipes printed on card and bound in a box wrapped in tartan ribbon. One of these was for Butterscotch Tart and gave the history of the name. Sadly, I loaned this to someone and never got it back but some believe that the name derives from a buttery toffee produced in Scotland a few centuries ago.

Ingredients:

2oz/55g butter

2 large eggs

1 pint/570ml milk

1 cup soft brown sugar

Vanilla essence

1 sachet gelatine

3 tbsp hot water

Preparation:

Melt butter and sugar and bring to the boil for 1 or 2 minutes, stirring continuously. Separate the eggs. Beat the yolks and add some of the milk. Stir into the butter mixture, gradually adding the remainder of milk. Add gelatine to the hot water mixing until it is completely melted. Bring the butter and milk mixture to boiling point, add the gelatine mixture and the vanilla. Leave to cool. Whip the egg whites until stiff and stir into the mixture. Pour into a serving dish and decorate with whipped cream and grated chocolate.

Marmalade Cake

Dundee in Scotland is famous for its marmalade but any homemade marmalade will suffice in this cake. The icing is also made with marmalade which gives the cake a pleasant tartness rather than making it oversweet.

Ingredients:

Cake:

6oz/170g soft margarine

10oz/285g self-raising flour

6oz/170g Dundee marmalade

3oz/85g golden syrup

5 tbsp fresh orange juice

2 eggs

2oz/55g sultanas

Topping:

3oz/85g butter

3oz/85g icing sugar

3oz/85g Dundee marmalade

Preparation:

Mix all cake ingredients together, beating until smooth. Pour into a greased cake tin and bake in a pre-heated oven at 350°F, 180°C, Gas mark 4 for approximately 35 minutes. Turn out onto a cooling tray. To make the topping, cream together the butter and sugar, mix in the marmalade and spread on top of the cake.

Huguenot Cake

The Huguenots were Protestants who were persecuted and expelled from France in the seventeenth century because of their faith. They fled to Europe and the Colonies, settling in large numbers in both Scotland (the Canongate area of Edinburgh) and Ulster (Lisburn, County Antrim), and the Appalachian region of South East America (South and North Carolina, Virginia, Tennessee and Kentucky). Many Ulster-Scots have Huguenot ancestors.

Ingredients:

Cake:

4 eggs

8oz/225g soft margarine

8oz/225g self-raising flour (sifted)

8oz/225g caster sugar

2 tsp baking powder

Filling:

10oz/285g stewed cooking apples (sugared to taste)

Topping:

½ pint/280ml whipping cream, whipped

2oz/55g walnuts, finely chopped

Preparation:

Beat eggs and margarine until light and fluffy then fold in the remaining ingredients with a metal spoon, being careful to keep as much air in the mixture as possible. Pour into a greased cake tin and bake in a pre-heated oven at 350°F, 180°C, Gas mark 4 for 35–40 minutes until the mixture springs up immediately when lightly pressed. Remove from the oven and when cool, slice the cake horizontally into two pieces. Sandwich together with the stewed apple mixture. Cover with whipped cream and sprinkle the walnuts on top.

Hairst Lemonade

A country lemon drink, traditionally taken at harvest time after a hard day's work in the fields gathering in the crops.

Ingredients:

¾ cup ground oatmeal

½ cup demerara sugar

2 lemons

Preparation:

Mix the oatmeal with a little warm water and add the sugar, juice and rind of the lemons. Add 1 gallon/4.5L of boiling water, stir thoroughly and leave to cool. Strain off the 'bits' and pour the lemonade into a jug. Serve chilled.

Plantation Punch (serves 6)

The following two recipes are versions of drinks from the American South – a punch and a sweet tea – both with an Ulster-Scots twist!

Ingredients:

1¼L Belfast Ale

300ml white rum

200ml lime juice

6 tbsp sugar syrup (melted sugar in water)

Crushed ice

Pineapple and lime slices to garnish

Preparation:

Mix the first four ingredients together in a large punch bowl, add the ice and fruit garnish. Chill and serve in individual glasses.

But gin it was right Nappy Beer,
Like it he by degrees wad clear,
And say, for seldom wad he swear,
Trouth its good ale.

William Starratt of Strabane, the Crochan Bard (eighteenth century)[14]

Sweet Apple Mint Tea (serves 2)

Ingredients:

2 cups boiling water

2 peppermint teabags

½ cup Bramley apple juice

1 tbsp Mourne Heather Honey

Pinch cinnamon

Preparation:

Pour the boiled water over the teabags in a teapot and steep for 10 minutes before discarding the teabags. Add the apple juice and honey and pour into cups. Add a pinch of cinnamon to each cup and stir.

My auld black pot is broke in two,
In which I did sae often brew,
The wee drap tea,
And thought it would ha'e cheer'd me through
Life's weary way.

Excerpt from 'The Auld Wife's Lament for her Teapot'
by David Herbison, Bard of Dunclug (1800–1880)[15]

CHAPTER 4

Weans' World

———⋅⊰≎⊱⋅———

Achanee, whun A was wee
A used tae sit on grannie's knee;
Her apron tore,
A fell tae tha floor,
Achanee, whun A was wee.

Traditional Ulster Rhyme[16]

{
This is a chapter dedicated to food for children
and is simply a collection of recipes I've used
or been given over the years, that appeal to the
weans – and us big kids, of course! Most have
been tried and tested on my two nephews and
have been given the thumbs up. Whenever
possible, I encourage the boys to help me prepare
and cook the food, and teach them about the
ingredients and cooking methods as we work
together. I try to make it fun and enjoy seeing
their wee faces when they proudly show off their
endeavours to their parents.
}

Rainbow Mackerel Toastie (serves 2)

This makes a healthy, crunchy sandwich filling for children, although the kidney beans can be left out if little noses are turned up at the thought!

Ingredients:

4 slices brown bread

Butter for spreading

2 mackerel fillets, cooked and flaked

1 tbsp red pepper, deseeded and finely chopped

1 tbsp kidney beans, drained

1 tbsp sweetcorn, drained

2 tbsp mayonnaise

Preparation:

Butter the bread. Rinse the kidney beans well in cold water. Mix the mackerel, mayo, pepper, beans and sweetcorn together and spread between the slices. Toast in a sandwich toaster or under the grill until golden.

Salmon Rollups

The first time I had these I was staying with our good friends, the Wilsons, who emigrated from Northern Ireland to Canada many years ago. Betty has given me great recipes over the years and these are some of my favourites. I've swapped the tuna used in the original recipe for salmon – it's more Ulster-Scots! A small tin should make about 4 rollups. It is important to remove the crusts from the bread as the finer the rollup, the easier for grilling.

Ingredients:

1 slice bread per person, crusts removed
Butter for spreading
1 salmon fillet, cooked and flaked
1 tbsp mayonnaise
Dash of Worcester Sauce
Cocktail sticks – 1 per rollup

Preparation:

Use a rolling pin to flatten out the bread slices. Butter the bread and mix the salmon with the mayo and sauce. Spread the mixture in the centre of the slice, roll it up and secure with a cocktail stick. Be careful not to use too much filling, or it will squish out the sides! Place rollups in the bottom of a grill pan, and toast under a low heat on both sides. Serve immediately.

Egg Rollups

Same as Salmon Rollups but replace the salmon with a hard-boiled, finely chopped egg mixed with mayo and a chopped scallion (spring onion). One egg should make 2–3 rollups.

Sausage and Apple Roll

This resembles a very large sausage roll when cooked and makes a tasty savoury addition to a birthday party or served with baked beans for tea.

Ingredients:

1 packet ready-made puff pastry

1 packet Ulster pork sausage meat

1 small Bramley apple, peeled, cored and thinly sliced

2 tbsp chutney

1 small egg, beaten

Preparation:

Roll the pastry out into a long rectangle and place on a greased baking sheet. Spread with the chutney. Shape the sausage into a long roll, until it almost fits the length of the pastry leaving about 1 inch/2.5cm from each end. Place the apple slices along the top of the sausage. Slice diagonally into the sides of the pastry with a sharp knife, keeping the same width between each slice. Dampen the edges of the pastry with cold water before rolling the pastry over the sausage and apple and using the cut sides to 'plait' the top of the pastry roll including the ends, until a log shape is created. Brush the log with the beaten egg and cook in a pre-heated oven at 350°F, 180°C, Gas mark 4 for 25–30 minutes until the pastry is crisp and golden.

A tub the youngsters quick procure,
And place, with water, on the floor:
Some little elves the apples drop,
Which lightly float upon the top.

Edward L Sloan, Bard of Conlig (1800s)[17]

Bangers and Mash with Fruity Onions

Bangers and Mash is usually a firm favourite with children and this recipe uses two of our best known produce – pork sausages and Comber spuds – with the addition of a homemade sweet onion sauce to give it a 'grown-up' feel!

Ingredients:

1lb/450g Ulster pork sausages

2lb/900g Comber potatoes, washed and peeled

1 tbsp Oakwood cheddar cheese, grated

pinch mild curry powder

1 tbsp sunflower oil

3 large onions, thinly sliced

1 tbsp soft brown sugar

115ml/4 fl oz pure orange juice

Seasoning

Preparation:

Boil the potatoes in salted water for 10–15 minutes, drain and mash with the cheese and curry powder. While the potatoes are cooking, grill the sausages and cook the onions by heating the oil in a saucepan, adding the onions and cooking gently for a few minutes until soft. Add juice, sugar and seasoning, and simmer for a further 10 minutes. Place the mash on the centre of the plate, poke the sausages into the mash and pour the onions over the sausages.

Sausages in the pan,
Sausages in the pan,
Turn them over
Turn them over,
Sausages in the pan.

Traditional skipping song[18]

Chicken and Plum Bake

If cooking a hot buffet for a family gathering, I like to include a special dish for the children even though we encourage them to eat what we eat. The following three recipes are quick and easy, yet contain local, fresh ingredients bound with a white sauce or, for real speed, tins of condensed soup – very useful store cupboard items when time is of the essence! The addition of crushed crisps as a topping is a compromise to breadcrumbs.

Ingredients:

1lb/450g chicken pieces

3 medium sized plums

1 tin condensed chicken soup

2 packets potato crisps, any flavour

Grated Coleraine cheddar cheese

Preparation:

Stone and slice the plums. Melt the butter in a frying pan and brown the chicken pieces on both sides. Place in a casserole dish and add the condensed soup. Top with the plum slices and crushed crisps, then the grated cheese. Bake in a pre-heated oven at 375°F, 190°C, Gas mark 5 for approximately 20–25 minutes.

Salmon and Mushroom Bake

Ingredients:

4 salmon fillets, cooked and flaked

1 packet potato crisps, any flavour

4oz/115g mushrooms, sliced

1 small onion, sliced

1oz/30g butter

1oz/30g plain flour

½pt/280ml milk

Seasoning

Preparation:

Crush half the packet of crisps into an ovenproof dish. Cover with salmon flakes. Add the onions and mushrooms. Make a white sauce by melting the butter over a low heat and adding the flour. Cook for 1 minute and slowly stir in the milk until the sauce thickens. Season to taste and pour over the onions and mushrooms. Cover with the remaining crisps and bake in a pre-heated oven at 350°F, 180°C, Gas mark 4 for 20–30 minutes.

Mackerel and Sweetcorn Bake

Sweetcorn is in season in Northern Ireland in September and October.

Ingredients:

4 mackerel fillets, cooked and flaked

2 cobs fresh sweetcorn, cooked and corn sliced off

(or 1 large can sweetcorn)

1 large can condensed mushroom soup

1 small onion, finely chopped

4 tbsp milk

3oz/85g uncooked pasta

3oz/85g breadcrumbs

3oz/85g grated Ulster cheddar

Preparation:

Mix together the mackerel, sweetcorn, onion, soup and milk, and spread over the base of an ovenproof dish. Layer the pasta, breadcrumbs and cheese and bake in a pre-heated oven at 350°F, 180°C, Gas mark 4 for 25–30 minutes.

Trifle Slabs (serves 6–8)

This is a great recipe for children's parties as it can be made the day before, looks colourful and is easy to serve. The fruit and jellies can be mixed and matched to suit individual tastes.

Ingredients:

1 large Raspberry Swiss Roll

1 tin Scottish raspberries

1 tin peaches

1 packet raspberry jelly

1 packet peach jelly

2 15oz/410g tins evaporated milk

½pt/280ml whipping cream

Chocolate buttons to decorate

Preparation:

Thinly slice the Swiss roll and line the bottom of a large square or rectangular Tupperware container. Drain the raspberries, reserving the juice and spread over the Swiss roll. Cut up the raspberry jelly cubes into a microwavable bowl and cover with the juice of the drained fruit and a little extra water if needed, until the cubes are covered. Melt in the microwave for about a minute on full power. Whisk in one tin of evaporated milk and pour the milky jelly over the fruit and the roll. Leave to set.

Make up the peach jelly in the same way but add the drained peaches to the jelly when melted, along with the second tin of milk, whisked. Pour over the set raspberry jelly and leave aside to set. Cut into squares and serve each with a dollop of whipped cream on top and a sprinkling of chocolate buttons.

Jelly on the plate,
Jelly on the plate,
Wibbly, wobbly
Wibbly, wobbly
Jelly on the plate.

Traditional Ulster Skipping Song[19]

Ice Cream

Who doesn't like ice-cream? I must admit, though, to be one of those people who only eats ice-cream if it isn't boring old vanilla! Having made my own ice-cream for the first time a few years ago, I now keep the recipe as a base for adding all kinds of flavours, particularly seasonal fruits, although if the *weans* prefer vanilla, use the basic recipe and add vanilla pods or essence. Here are two fruity favourites.

RHUBARB AND GINGER

Ingredients:

½ pt/280ml milk

4oz/115g caster sugar

3 eggs, lightly beaten

1lb/450g fresh rhubarb

1 level tsp ground ginger

1 pt/570ml double cream, whipped

Preparation:

Wash the rhubarb and slice into chunks. Place in a saucepan with the ginger and half of the sugar, and bring to the boil. Simmer for 10–15 minutes until the rhubarb is soft. Drain off any surplus liquid and leave to cool.

Place the remaining sugar, milk and eggs in a bowl over a pan of simmering water and stir continuously until the mixture covers the back of the spoon. When cool, pour into a large plastic container (with a lid) and freeze for 1 hour.

Remove from the freezer and whisk to break up any ice granules. Add the rhubarb and ginger mixture and mix well. Return to the freezer until firm. Remove and whisk in the whipped double cream. Return to the freezer until firm. Remove from the freezer approximately 15–20 minutes before serving to soften the ice cream, making it easier to scoop into tall glasses.

GOOSEBERRY AND ELDERFLOWER

Elderflowers are found in local hedgerows during the summer. If out of season, use 6 tbsp of elderflower cordial instead of the syrup.

Ingredients:

½ pt/280ml milk

4oz/115g caster sugar

3 eggs, lightly beaten

1lb/450g fresh gooseberries

1 pt/570ml double cream, whipped

Elderflower Syrup:

4–5 elderflower heads

3oz/85g caster sugar

½ pt/280ml water

Preparation:

Make the elderflower syrup by placing the flower heads in a saucepan with the sugar and water. Bring to the boil and simmer for 10 minutes. Leave the flowers in the syrup to cool before straining – this will bring out the flavour.

Top and tail the gooseberries. Place in a saucepan with half of the sugar and bring to the boil. Simmer for 10–15 minutes until the fruit is soft. Drain off any surplus liquid and leave to cool.

Place the remaining sugar, milk and eggs in a bowl over a pan of simmering water and stir continuously until the mixture covers the back of the spoon. When cool, pour into a large plastic container (with a lid) and freeze for 1 hour.

Remove from the freezer and whisk to break up any ice granules. Add the gooseberries and elderflower syrup and mix well. Return to the freezer until firm. Remove and whisk in the whipped double cream. Return to the freezer until firm. Remove from the freezer approximately 15–20 minutes before serving to soften the ice cream, making it easier to scoop into tall glasses.

Breid 'n' Butther Pudding (serves 6)

Here's a recipe for turning bread and milk into something much tastier – a bread and butter pudding, Ulster-Scots style – using traditional Ulster fruit bread. If you want to make an adult version, soak the sultanas in whisky rather than orange juice!

Ingredients:

10 slices of Barmbrack (a traditional Ulster fruit loaf)
Butter for spreading
2oz/55g sultanas, soaked in orange juice for at least 30 minutes
3 large eggs
2oz/55g soft brown sugar
10 fl oz/280ml milk
2½ fl oz/60ml double cream

Preparation:

Butter bread and cut the slices into triangular pieces. Arrange in a greased baking dish in layers, alternating each layer with the drained sultanas. Lightly whisk together the milk, cream and sugar. Whisk the eggs in a separate bowl and gently add to the milk mixture. Pour over the bread and let the pudding sit for about half an hour to absorb the liquid. Bake in a pre-heated oven at 350°F, 180°C, Gas mark 4 for 30–40 minutes until golden. Ideally, the pudding should be shooglin aboot (wobbly) when lifting it out – you don't want it too stodgy.

Up Hard Breid Raa
A lost ma Da
An whaur dae ye think A found him?
Behind tha pump
Scobin' his rump
Wi aa tha weans aroon him.

Traditional Ulster Song[20]

My Mum's Trio of Traybakes

Traditionally, home baking played an important part in the Ulster-Scots kitchen with the making of bread, cakes, buns and biscuits. Recipes were handed down from generation to generation or exchanged between friends but this tradition has sadly been in decline over the past few decades – time, cost, and dieting being major factors. It is a great shame as, in my humble opinion, homemade tastes so much better, and is healthier, than shop-bought produce.

The next three recipes are for traybakes (buns or biscuits made in trays and cut into squares) which my mum made for us when we were children. These are from the 1960s when she regularly met friends for coffee mornings and swapped recipes. I usually make a batch of these for freezing just a few weeks before Christmas, although by the time Christmas arrives there aren't many left!

PEPPERMINT SQUARES

Ingredients:

Base:

4oz/115g soft margarine

2oz/55g caster sugar

4oz/115g plain flour

1 tsp baking powder

2oz/55g coconut

1oz/30g cocoa

Centre:

4oz/115g soft margarine

8oz/225g icing sugar

few drops green colouring

4–6 drops peppermint essence

Topping:

1oz/30g soft margarine

6oz/170g plain chocolate

Preparation:

For the base, cream the margarine and caster sugar together, before adding the rest of ingredients to the mixture. Spread onto a greased traybake tin and bake in a pre-heated oven at 350°F, 180°C, Gas mark 4 for 20 minutes. Remove from the oven and leave to cool.

For the filling, cream the margarine and icing sugar together before adding the colouring and essence to taste. Spread over the cooked base.

For the topping, melt the chocolate and soft margarine together either in the microwave or in a bowl over a pan of simmering water. Make sure that the bottom of the bowl doesn't touch the water. When melted, spread over the peppermint mixture and leave to set before cutting into squares.

CARAMEL SQUARES

Ingredients:

Base:

8oz/225g soft margarine

4oz/115g caster sugar

10oz/285g plain flour

Centre:

4oz/115g caster sugar

4 tbsp golden syrup

14oz/400g can sweetened condensed milk

Topping:

1oz/30g soft margarine

8oz/225g milk chocolate

Preparation:

For the base, cream the margarine and sugar together and mix in the flour until soft dough is formed. Press into a greased baking tray and prick well with a fork. Bake in a pre-heated oven at 350°F, 180°C, Gas mark 4 for 30 minutes until crisp and golden.

For the filling, put all the ingredients into a saucepan and stir over a low heat until melted. Bring to the boil, cook for 3–5 minutes until golden and thick and a caramel is formed. Spread over the cooked base and leave to set.

For the topping, melt chocolate and margarine together either in the microwave or in a saucepan over a low heat. Spread over the filling and leave to set. Cut into squares.

LEMON SQUARES

Ingredients:

4oz/115g soft margarine

Small tin sweetened condensed milk

8oz/225g packet digestive biscuits, crushed

4oz/115g desiccated coconut

Topping:

12oz/340g icing sugar

1 lemon

Preparation:

Melt margarine and condensed milk together in a saucepan. Add the crushed biscuits and coconut, and stir until blended. Pour into a baking tray and leave to cool. Grate the lemon and set the rind aside. Put the icing sugar into a bowl and mix into a paste with the juice of the lemon. Pour the icing over the biscuit base, sprinkle with the lemon rind and leave to set before cutting into squares.

Traffic Lights

These are super for a children's birthday party as they can clearly see the resemblance with the use of red, 'amber' and green cherries. However, sometimes it's difficult to find the coloured cherries, so if using red, rename the traybakes 'Rudolph's Nose' or whatever your imagination dreams up!

Ingredients:

12oz/340g milk chocolate

6oz/170g crushed oatmeal biscuits

14oz/397g tin sweetened condensed milk

Red, green and yellow glacé cherries

Preparation:

Melt the chocolate and milk in a large saucepan, and stir in the crushed biscuits. Pour into a greased baking tray and leave to set. Cut into fingers and decorate with cherries, 3 per finger – red, yellow, then green for the traffic lights!

County Antrim Cookies

I found this recipe inside a hymn book in a Presbyterian Church in Bushmills, County Antrim. We sometimes attended the service here when on holiday in this stunningly beautiful area of the North Antrim Coast. It was written in an elegant hand on a scrap of paper!

Ingredients:

4oz/115g oatmeal

4oz/115g self-raising flour

6oz/170g soft margarine

4oz/115g caster sugar

1 small egg, beaten

2 cups cornflakes, crushed

½ cup coconut

Caster sugar for coating

Glacé cherries

Preparation:

Cream together margarine and sugar. Add the beaten egg and other dry ingredients. Roll the mixture into small balls, dip in the extra sugar and place well apart on a greased baking tray. Place a halved cherry on top of each and bake in a pre-heated oven at 375°F, 190°C, Gas mark 5 for 30 minutes.

CHAPTER 5

Carry on Caravanning

———◆———

It was not worth your while;
To sup on buttermilk and slugs
And lie on chaffy hammock,
Beneath our coarse-grained country rugs
Would suit but ill your stomach.

Samuel Thomson, the Bard of Carngranny (1766–1816)[21]

{ When I was young, my family spent many
summer holidays caravanning in Newcastle and
Millisle in County Down, and Portrush in County
Antrim. Food needed to be easily transported
and easily constructed as the kitchens were small,
and we often picnicked on the beach and in forest
country parks. Sometimes we would be joined
by friends and there would be a large gathering
on the beach at White Rocks in Portrush with
everyone contributing to the overall meal,
making for some unusual but tasty recipes. I
remember one summer in Bushmills, during
the Twelfth of July Parades, when a group of us
spread a travel rug on the footpath and proceeded
to set out and eat our picnic lunch whilst cheering
on the bands, much to the amusement of the
Orangemen! }

Our Favourite Sarnies (serves 2, i.e. 8 triangles)

I come from a long line of Presbyterians and my granny was a member of the Women's Guild, the Presbyterian Church's equivalent of the Women's Institute. During the early 1600s there were three ways of denoting the Ulster-Scots settlements – by their language, by their surnames, and by their Presbyterianism. The Women's Guild was often required to organise catering for church functions and I had my first taste of 'mock crab' sandwiches at one such event!

SALMON AND WORCESTER

Ingredients:

2 fresh salmon fillets, cooked

2 scallions

Dollop of mayonnaise

Dash of Worcestershire sauce

Preparation:

Flake the salmon fillets into a bowl and mix with the mayo, chopped scallions and sauce.

MOCK CRAB

Ingredients:

Knob of butter

½ small onion, finely chopped

1 tomato, finely chopped

2 small eggs

Grated cheddar cheese

Preparation:

Melt the butter in a saucepan and cook the onion and tomato for 2 minutes. Break the eggs into the saucepan and stir continuously over a low heat until the eggs are cooked and look slightly 'scrambled.' Stir in enough grated cheese to make a spreadable consistency.

LUNCHEON MEAT WITH ONION AND TOMATO

A tin of pork and ham luncheon meat was a handy and inexpensive way to produce a tasty sandwich filling.

Ingredients:

2 small tins pork and ham luncheon meat
1 tomato, finely chopped
½ small onion, finely chopped

Preparation:

Mix and spread! Seriously, this does make a tasty filling!

Ulster-Scotch Eggs

A bit tongue-in-cheek! I love Scotch eggs and learned how to make them in school. This is the same recipe using local ingredients.

Ingredients:

4 Ulster farm fresh eggs

12oz/340g Ulster pork sausagemeat

2 tbsp parsley, finely chopped

1oz/30g plain flour, seasoned with salt and pepper

1 egg, beaten

4oz/115g very fine breadcrumbs

Vegetable oil for deep frying

Preparation:

Boil eggs for 10 minutes. Cool and remove shells. Add the parsley to the sausagemeat and mix through. Using your fingers, mould the sausagemeat around the eggs. Roll in flour, dip into beaten egg and roll in breadcrumbs. Fry in very hot oil until golden. Drain on kitchen paper and serve hot or cold.

Fresh Tomato and Vegetable Soup (serves 6)

On our infamous picnics, one family would bring a large tin of vegetable soup and another, a large tin of tomato soup and we'd mix these together and heat over a single ring gas stove. Here's my own recipe for the same flavours using fresh local ingredients.

Ingredients:

2 tbsp sunflower oil

1 large onion, sliced

1 large clove garlic, finely chopped

1lb/450g tomatoes

3 carrots, sliced

2 sticks celery, chopped

1 large leek, sliced

2 parsnips, sliced

2 pts/1.1L vegetable stock

Seasoning

Fresh basil, torn

Preparation:

Put the oil and garlic in a large saucepan, and turn on the heat. Fry the garlic gently but don't let it burn. Add the onions, partially cover with lid and let these sweat for approximately 2 minutes. Add the carrots, leeks, celery and parsnips, and continue cooking, stirring all the time until the vegetables are coated in the oil. Add the stock and seasoning, bring to the boil and simmer for 20 minutes.

Meanwhile, put the tomatoes in a heatproof bowl and cover with boiling water. Cover with a clean tea towel and leave for 10 minutes. Remove from the bowl using a fork and peel the skin, which should have split allowing for easy removal, but don't be too fussy about taking off all the skin. Chop the tomatoes and using a hand held blender or food processor, blend until smooth. Add to the soup with the basil and continue cooking for a further 10 minutes. Adjust the seasoning if required and serve piping hot.

Orangeman's Soup (serves 6)

This soup is reminiscent of my caravanning summers and the annual Twelfth of July Orange Order Parades, when the weather was either gloriously hot or gloomily wet. The Twelfth holidays have been an important tradition in my life, watching my grandpa march along the route in his black, red and gold uniform, playing saxophone in the Ormeau Military Band, a band formed (c.1920 as Ormeau Flute Band) and conducted by my great-grandfather, James Bell. As many members of the Grand Orange Lodge of Ireland are of Ulster-Scots descent, I dedicate this soup to all Orangemen and Bandsmen at home and abroad, who may have welcomed a cup at the end of a long damp march!

Ingredients:

2 tbsp oil
2 medium onions, chopped
3 large carrots, sliced
2 leeks, sliced
4oz/115g orange lentils
2pt/1.1L chicken stock
Seasoning
Parsley, chopped

Preparation:

Heat the oil in a large saucepan and add the chopped onions. Cook for 5 minutes, stirring occasionally. Add the carrots and leeks, and cook for a further 5 minutes. Stir in the lentils and stock. Season, bring to the boil and simmer for 35–40 minutes, stirring occasionally to make sure the lentils don't stick to the bottom – add more water if necessary. Liquidise in a food processor or use a hand-blender. Add parsley and serve.

Ulster-Scots Stew (serves 6)

Stew is a great standby for caravanning as it can be made the night before leaving home and transported in the saucepan it was cooked in, heated up when you arrive and served with little fuss. I concocted this recipe for an Ulster-Scots Summer School in Belfast where I was taking a cookery workshop. I used potatoes as the staple ingredient but added bacon rather than the traditional lamb or beef, thus reducing stewing time. Gammon can also be used but will take slightly longer to cook.

Ingredients:

1 tbsp sunflower oil
8 rashers Ulster smoked back bacon, cut into strips
(or 1lb 6oz/750g smoked gammon joint, cooked and cut into cubes)
8 medium Comber potatoes, washed, peeled and thinly sliced
1 large onion, sliced
1pt/570ml chicken stock
Seasoning
Brown sauce
Parsley, roughly chopped

Preparation:

Fry the potatoes in the oil for 3–4 minutes. If using gammon, cook the joint according to the instructions on the packet. Add the bacon or gammon and onions, and fry for another 2–3 minutes until the onions are soft. Add the stock and a dash of brown sauce, and taste before seasoning as the bacon will probably be very salty. Simmer over a low heat for 20–25 minutes (30–35 minutes for the gammon) or until the potatoes are cooked. Add chopped parsley and serve with toasted, buttered soda bread.

Sure some kind deel has brought us
Yon yellow chief, that taught us
To cleek the tythe potatoes
Frae ilk a greedy gown!

Frae 'Scotch Poems' from East Donegal in 1753 (Anon)[22]

Trout with Watercress Sauce

The following three recipes cook the fresh fish over a barbeque, although an ordinary grill is fine. My family have a caravan at Cloughey in County Down and make great use of the barbeque during the long summer evenings.

Ingredients:

4 trout fillets

6oz/170g butter, softened

Salt and black pepper

Sauce:

1 packet watercress

½ lemon (juice)

7floz/200ml crème fraiche

Seasoning

Preparation:

Shape 4 pieces of foil into a 'boat' shape, suitable for holding one piece of fish. Spread half of the butter over each 'boat' and place one fillet in each. Make slits diagonally along the skin of each fish, season, and cover with remaining butter. Cook over a hot barbecue (or under a grill) for about 10–15 minutes, turning the fish once in the 'boat' during cooking.

To make the sauce, put the ingredients in a liquidiser and blend. Pour into a saucepan and gently heat through.

Mackerel with Gussgab Sauce

Gussgab is Ulster-Scots for gooseberry.

Ingredients:

4 mackerel fillets

6oz/170g butter, softened

Salt and black pepper

Sauce:

80z/225g gussgabs (gooseberries), topped and tailed

3 tbsp dry cider

1oz/30g butter

1 tbsp caster sugar

Preparation:

Cook the mackerel in the same way as the trout in the previous recipe.

To make the sauce, mix the gooseberries, cider and butter together in a saucepan and simmer until the fruit is soft. Puree with a hand held blender and add the sugar. Pour into a sauceboat, ready to serve.

I hae mine o' sellin' mackerel tae a wummin' wee an' stout;
She seem't tae be as broad as she wus lang.
Oot she land't wae a basin for tae houl the stripp'it fish,
An' the wains al follied efter in a thrang.

Charlie Gillen, contemporary Ulster-Scots poet[23]

Oaty Herrings with Apple Chutney

Portavogie harbour in County Down is one of Northern Ireland's principle fishing ports, its main catch being prawns and herrings. Portavogie has a large Ulster-Scots population and is home to the excellent Portavogie Fishermen's Choir.

Ingredients:

4 herrings, filleted

Oil to baste

4 tbsp porridge oats

Salt and black pepper

Chutney: 2 Armagh Bramley apples, peeled and cored

2 red onions, finely chopped

8 cherry tomatoes, halved

3 tbsp brown sugar

2 tbsp white wine vinegar

¼pt/140ml white wine

½ tsp ground ginger

Knob of butter

Preparation:

Cook the herrings in the same way as the trout but coat each fillet by dipping first in the oil, then the oats, before cooking for 2–3 minutes on each side or until golden.

To make the chutney, cut the apples into chunks. Melt the butter in a saucepan and fry the onion until softened, being careful not to let it brown. Add the rest of the ingredients, bring to the boil and simmer for 45 minutes or until the chutney has thickened. Drain off any excess liquid. Leave to cool and serve with the herring.

As for the pay I will not speak,
I only earned one bob a week
'Twould scarcely buy a herring and leek
For the poor weaver ...

Robert Donnelly, nineteenth century rhyming weaver poet[24]

Chicken Drumsticks with Tennessee BBQ Sauce (serves 8)

Many Southern States have their own BBQ sauce recipe. This one is adapted from Tennessee, where many Ulster-Scots settled in the eighteenth century.

Ingredients:

8 Chicken drumsticks

Seasoning

Butter for basting

Sauce:

1 tbsp oil

1 onion, finely chopped

1 clove garlic, crushed and finely chopped

½ tsp crushed red pepper flakes

½ cup tomato sauce

½ cup pure orange juice

½ cup whiskey

1 tbsp soft brown sugar

1 tsp mustard powder

1 tsp Worcester sauce

1 tsp grated orange rind

Preparation:

Spread the butter over the drumsticks and season. Cook the chicken on the barbeque or under a grill for 10–15 minutes on each side until the skin is crisp and the chicken is cooked right through. Use a knife to press down on the drumstick and if the juice runs clear, the chicken should be cooked. If in doubt, cut a little way into the drumstick to make sure.

To make the BBQ sauce, heat oil in a saucepan. Add onions, garlic, and red pepper flakes, and cook for 5 minutes until soft. Add tomato sauce, orange juice, whiskey, brown sugar, mustard, Worcester sauce, and orange rind. Simmer for 30 minutes, stirring occasionally. Pour over the drumsticks and serve immediately.

Dulse (Seaweed) Champ

As a child I remember taking my fishing net to the rock pools in Portrush to do a spot of 'dulse' fishing. Dulse is still sold today at the Auld Lammas Fair, Northern Ireland's oldest market fair which takes place every August in Ballycastle, County Antrim. Amongst the street entertainment, traditional music and market stalls, two traditional foods are sold – dulse, an edible seaweed, and Yellow Man, a golden crunchy toffee.

Did you treat your Mary Ann to some
dulse and yellowman,
At the Auld Lammas Fair in Ballycastle-O?

Traditional Ulster Song[25]

CHAMP (BASIC)

Champ or creamed potatoes is another favourite Ulster-Scots dish. It is traditional to boil the scallions in a little milk and add these to the mash, but I hate damp scallions so add them raw – this makes the dish crunchy and you'll get more flavour from the scallions.

Ingredients:

2lb/900g potatoes
Ground pepper
1/4pt/140ml single cream
4oz/115g butter
8 scallions (spring onions)

Preparation:

Wash and peel the potatoes. Boil in salted water until cooked (about 15 minutes), drain and mash with the butter, cream and pepper. Add the scallions, finely chopped.

DULSE

Preparation:

Soak about two gowpins (handfuls) of dry dulse in fresh water for about an hour. Drain and simmer gently in milk for about 30 minutes or until tender. Drain and add to the champ instead of the scallions.

Yellow Man

Ingredients:

1 oz/30g butter

2 tbsp/30ml water

1lb/450g golden syrup

8oz/225g caster sugar

1 tsp baking soda

Preparation:

In a large heavy-based saucepan, melt the butter and add water, sugar and syrup. Stir over a low heat until dissolved. Boil unstirred for about 5 minutes until caramelised. Test by dropping a small amount in cold water – it's ready if the mixture becomes 'crispy'. Stir in the baking soda and pour into a large greased dish. When completely set, cut into chunks.

Here's yellow-man, an' tuffy sweet,
Girls will ye taste or pree it.

Robert Huddleston, Bard of Moneyreagh (1800s)[26]

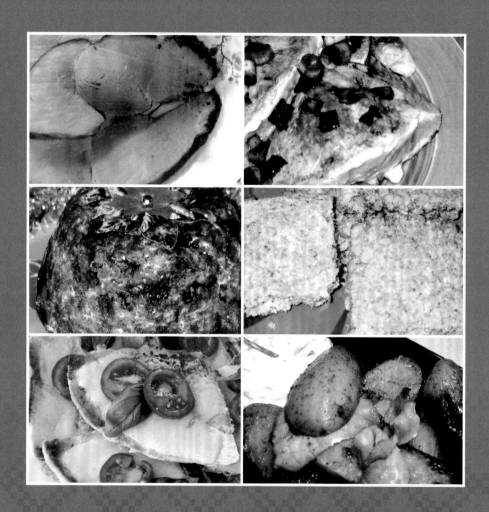

CHAPTER 6

A Blythe Yuletide

⚬───◇◇───⚬

Christmas is coming,
And the goose is getting fat.
Please put a penny in tha oul man's hat.
If ye hinnae got a penny,
A ha'penny will do,
If ye hinnae got a ha'penny,
Then God Bless YOU!

Traditional Ulster Street Rhyme[27]

{
**The final chapter covers one of my favourite times
of year – Christmas. It's a time for tradition,
eating good food, and relaxing with my family.**

A blithe Yuletide an a guid Neu Yeir tae yin an aa!
}

Strangford Lough Queenies with Warm Bacon Salad

Strangford Lough is the biggest sea lough in the British Isles. We refer to Queen Scallops as Queenies.

Ingredients:

4 Queen Scallops per person

4 tbsp olive oil

Salad leaves – rocket, baby spinach and watercress

8 scallions, shredded

8 rashers Ulster bacon, chopped

Juice of a lemon

Juice of a lime

Sea salt and black pepper

Preparation:

Place the leaves onto individual serving plates and add the scallions. Rinse the scallops in cold water, pat dry with kitchen paper and season both sides. Add a little of the oil to a frying pan and add the chopped bacon. Cook for 1–2 minutes before adding the scallops. Cook the scallops for no longer than 1–2 minutes each side (being very careful not to overcook them or they will be rubbery), then drain both bacon and scallops on kitchen paper before placing them on the leaves. Add the remaining oil with the lemon and lime juices to the frying pan, and quickly warm through. Season with black pepper and pour over the scallops and leaves. Serve immediately.

Field Mushrooms with Ballyblue and Cranberry Stuffing

I had something similar to this in a local restaurant a few years ago and attempted to make it at home. Any type of local cheese can be used but don't forgo the cranberry sauce as the sweetness makes this dish.

Ingredients:

4 large flat field mushrooms

½ onion, finely chopped

2oz/55g breadcrumbs

2oz/55g Ballyblue soft cheese

2oz/55g cranberry sauce

2oz/55g butter

3 tbsp olive oil

Salt and pepper

Preparation:

Wipe the mushrooms, take off the stalks and chop finely. Melt 1oz/30g butter with 1 tbsp of the oil in a frying pan, add the onion and mushroom stalks and stir over a moderate heat for about 5 minutes. Remove from the heat and stir in the remaining oil and breadcrumbs, and season to taste.

Place the mushroom tops in a well-oiled ovenproof dish and divide the cranberry sauce amongst each mushroom. Spread the cheese over the cranberry sauce. Spoon the breadcrumb mixture over the top of the cheese and dot with the remaining butter. Bake in a pre-heated oven at 350°F, 180°C, Gas mark 4 for about 25 minutes.

Smoked Salmon and Ginger Rollups

My family and I are, or have been, members of local choirs and operatic companies throughout the years. Usually, if performing at a church venue, a supper is provided by the ladies of the congregation and, sorry to the townies, the *countryins* produce some of the best home cooking I've tasted! I had this very upmarket sandwich at a supper after a choir concert many years ago and it was super.

Ingredients:

8 slices of Veda bread

Butter for spreading

8 slices smoked salmon

2oz/55g cream cheese

2oz/55g crystallised ginger

Preparation:

Remove the crusts of the bread and flatten with a rolling pin. Mix the cheese with the ginger.

Butter the bread and place a piece of smoked salmon on each slice, and cover with the cheese mixture. Roll up and secure with a cocktail stick. Serve 2 rollups per person on a bed of mixed leaves for a simple yet tasty starter.

Christmas Goose with Apple Stuffing and Port Sauce (serves 6–8)

I deliberately didn't include the traditional Christmas turkey as most people already have a favourite way of cooking it. When I was wee, we always had Christmas dinner at granny and grandpas' and it was a truly magical time. I remember the turkey came from a farm and was hung by its feet on the scullery door until granny plucked it. I can still remember the sound of the feathers being torn from the bird in an upward motion, and the sight of those gnarled feet!

We have always stuffed our turkeys, chickens, etc without any problem but if you are wary of putting the stuffing inside the bird, place in a separate ovenproof dish and dot with butter. Cook alongside the bird for approximately 30 minutes. In this case, stuff the bird with a lemon, an orange and an apple, if room. These will help to flavour and moisten the bird and can be thrown away when the bird is cooked.

Ingredients:

1 medium goose (about 4.5kg/10lbs)

1 lemon

Stuffing:

1 cup breadcrumbs

1 cup finely chopped onion

2 tbsp finely chopped Bramley apple

1 tbsp finely chopped parsley

1 tsp finely chopped sage

1 tbsp butter, melted

Seasoning

Sauce:

1 cup Port

1 tbsp butter

Preparation:

Remove the innards and clean the goose by rinsing well under running water, then pat dry with kitchen roll. Cut the lemon and rub the inside of the goose with the cut parts. Make the stuffing by mixing the breadcrumbs, onion, apple and herbs with the melted butter and season to taste. Stuff the neck end of the goose and use a metal skewer to secure the stuffing. Place in a roasting pan and season with salt and freshly ground black pepper. Roast in a pre-heated oven at 325°F, 160°C, Gas mark 3 for approximately 3 hours, turning halfway through. Baste throughout the cooking time and test if cooked by pressing the bird with the back of a spoon or sticking a skewer into the breast and leg areas. If blood runs out, the bird will need 15–20 minutes extra cooking. When cooked, remove from the oven and place on a carving plate. Leave to stand for about 10 minutes to ensure the juices run through the bird.

To make the gravy, pour the port into the roasting pan and bring to the boil, scraping the 'bits' from the bottom of the pan. Allow to boil for a few minutes, stirring until the port is reduced and the sauce thickens. Stir in the butter until the sauce becomes 'glazed' and adjust the seasoning if necessary. Drain the 'bits' through a sieve and pour the sauce into a gravy boat ready to serve with the goose.

Baked Belfast Ham with Antrim Sauce
(serves 6–8)

My granny would bake or boil her own ham with leftovers being turned into a ham salad or ham sandwiches for the following day. This recipe coats the ham in sweet honey and wine, the flavours of which are repeated in the accompanying Antrim sauce.

Ingredients:

10lb/4.5kg Belfast Ham

1 tbsp whole cloves

1 cup Madeira wine

4 tbsp Mourne Heather Honey

Sauce:

1 small onion, finely chopped

8oz/225g butter

1 cup plain flour

2 cups water

1 level tsp mustard powder

1 tsp demerara sugar

1 tbsp tomato purée

1 cup Madeira wine

Preparation:

Soak the ham in a large pan of cold water overnight to get rid of as much salt as possible. Drain, then re-cover with fresh water and bring to the boil before simmering for about 2 hours. Drain, place ham in a roasting dish and score the skin diagonally each way with a sharp knife. Stud the surface with the cloves, drizzle over the honey and wine, and bake in a pre-heated oven at 350°F, 180°C, Gas mark 4 for 2½ hours. Remove from the oven and leave to rest for 10 minutes. Slice and serve with the Antrim Sauce.

To make the sauce, lightly sauté the onion in the butter, mix in the flour and stir until blended. Cook for 1 minute before adding the water. Blend and simmer for 15 minutes. Add puree, mustard, sugar and wine, and simmer for a further 10 minutes. Season to taste.

Boyne Salmon with Ginger and Scallion Sauce

The Boyne River is in the Republic of Ireland and is the location of a famous battle celebrated annually on the Twelfth of July in Northern Ireland and in some parts of the Republic. William III's (King Billy's) army defeated that of James II and although the battle was fought on 1st July 1690, the adoption of the Gregorian calendar altered the date to that of the 12th. Ulster-Scots fought on the side of both Williamites and Jacobites. There are also Boyne Rivers in Canada, Australia, and the United States of America where many Ulster-Scots settled during the eighteenth century.

Ingredients:

4 salmon fillets

2oz/55g butter

Sea salt and black pepper

1 large clove garlic, finely chopped

8 tbsp light soy sauce

1 tsp lemon juice

6 scallions, finely chopped

1inch/2.5cm ginger root, finely grated

Preparation:

Mix the garlic, soy sauce, lemon juice, scallions and ginger in a bowl. Season the salmon and pan fry the fillets in the butter for about 10 minutes until the skin is crispy and the fish has a little 'give' when pressed. Add the sauce mixture and heat through. Serve with a green salad or new potatoes and broccoli.

Roasted Honey and Garlic Vegetables

There is nothing better to accompany a Sunday roast dinner than vegetables fresh from the greengrocer or, if we're lucky, from our own garden. Carrots, swedes, cabbages and cauliflowers are in season all year round in Northern Ireland.

Ingredients:

Selection of vegetables, i.e. carrots, parsnips, swedes, courgettes

Mourne Heather Honey

Garlic cloves, finely chopped

Butter and olive oil for roasting

Salt and black pepper

Preparation:

Wash and peel the vegetables. Cut into chunks and boil in salted water for 2–3 minutes only. Drain and place in a roasting pan. Season, sprinkle over the garlic, drizzle over the honey, dot with the butter and pour in the oil. Shake the pan to coat the vegetables and roast in a pre-heated oven at 350°F, 180°C, Gas mark 4 for 50 minutes to an hour until cooked.

Mustard Roasted Potatoes

A staple diet in Northern Ireland, the potato, or *prouta* in Ulster-Scots, is in season all year round. This recipe for roast potatoes adds mustard powder to flour to give the spuds a 'kick'.

Ingredients:

4 large potatoes

2oz/55g plain flour

1oz/30g mustard powder

Seasoning

Oil for roasting

Preparation:

Wash and peel the potatoes. Boil in salted water for 2–3 minutes. Drain and place on a tea towel to dry and cool. Mix the flour, mustard powder and seasoning together on a large plate and roll the potatoes in this until well coated. Place in a roasting pan, drizzle with oil and roast in a pre-heated oven at 350°F, 180°C, Gas mark 4 for 50 minutes to an hour until cooked.

Did ye iver in the ashes
Roast a prata ye had dug?
Did ye ate it lake a banquet?
Wur ye blak fae ear tae lug?

Charlie Gillen, contemporary Ulster-Scots poet[28]

Clementine and Cinnamon Pavlova

My relatives often regale us at Christmas with tales of what they found in their Christmas stockings as *weans* – shiny pennies, boiled sweets and Clementine oranges, etc! I decided therefore to use Clementines and cinnamon to give this pavlova recipe a really Christmassy scent and flavour.

Ingredients:

3 large egg whites

6oz/170g caster sugar

1 tsp vinegar

1 tsp cornflour

1 tbsp cinnamon

3 Clementine oranges

½ pt/280ml double cream

Dark chocolate, grated for decoration

Preparation:

Place a 9inch/23cm circle of tin foil onto a baking sheet, shiny side up. Beat the egg whites until stiff. Whisk in half of the sugar until blended and gradually add remaining sugar, mixing well between each addition. Fold in the vinegar, cinnamon and cornflour. Spoon mixture onto the foil and bake in a pre-heated oven at 300°F, 150°C, Gas mark 2 for approximately 1 hour. Leave to cool in the oven before turning out onto a serving plate. Whip the cream and pile it on top of the meringue. Decorate with peeled clementines and grated chocolate.

Ulster-Scots Trifle (serves 6–8)

Christmas dinner wouldn't be complete in our house without trifle to follow. This recipe is a boozy one but you can substitute the whisky with fresh orange juice if you prefer. Creamy homemade custard is so much better than shop bought, but if stuck for time, buy a good quality custard. The toasted oats and honey topping makes an interesting change.

Ingredients:

1 packet trifle sponges

4 tbsp Bushmills Whisky

12oz/340g fresh Scottish raspberries

1oz/30g caster sugar

Custard:

1 pint/570ml full cream milk

½ vanilla pod

2 eggs

2 egg yolks

2 tbsp caster sugar

Topping:

½pint/280ml double cream

1oz/30g toasted oats

2 tsp Mourne Heather Honey

Preparation:

Slice the trifle sponges in half lengthways and arrange around the bottom and sides of a large glass bowl. Pour over the whisky. Place the raspberries on top and sprinkle with the sugar.

Make the custard by bringing the milk and vanilla pod to the boil in a saucepan. Remove from the heat and leave to cool. Beat the eggs and egg yolks together with the sugar, remove the vanilla pod from the milk and stir the sugar mixture into the milk. Return to a low heat, stirring continuously until the mixture thickens. Cool slightly and pour over the raspberries. Lightly whip the cream and spread over the custard. Sprinkle the toasted oats and drizzle the honey over the top.

Cranachan (traditional Scottish dessert) (Serves 6–8)

It is traditional in Scotland to set the table with the individual ingredients and let the guests assemble their own dessert according to taste. Any malt whisky can be used but for this recipe I chose Bladnoch's, which is from a grain whisky distillery in Galloway, one of three remaining grain distilleries in the Lowlands of Scotland, the land of our forefathers.

Ingredients:

15 fl oz/425ml double cream, whipped

4oz/115g coarse or pinhead oatmeal, lightly toasted

8oz/225g soft cheese or crème fraiche

1lb/450g soft fruit (e.g. raspberries, strawberries, loganberries or tayberries)

Mourne Heather Honey to taste

Bladnoch whisky to taste

Preparation:

In a large serving bowl, mix the cream and cheese together until well blended. Sprinkle with the oatmeal and add the fruit and honey. Pour the whisky over the mixture and stir through. Adjust honey and whisky measures as required.

Drank out the whiskey every seep,
And down the bicker set.

Samuel Thomson, Bard of Carngranny (1766–1816)[29]

Tayberry and Plum Fool

The tayberry is a sweet red berry, a cross between a raspberry and a blackberry. It is commonly grown on farms around Counties Down and Antrim during the summer. You can still use the tayberry out of season either by making your own tayberry jam in autumn or freezing the fresh fruit for the winter. Defrost overnight in the fridge in a plastic container and as the fruit loses its sugar through freezing, the addition of honey or sugar is essential to replenish the sweetness.

Ingredients:

8oz/225g tayberries

4 medium plums

2oz/55g soft brown sugar

15oz/425g natural yoghurt

¼pt/140ml double cream

Chocolate shavings

Shortbread fingers

Preparation:

Wash the fruit and stone the plums. Cut the plums into chunks and place in a saucepan with the tayberries and sugar. Simmer gently for 8–10 minutes until the fruit is softened. Blend in a liquidiser or food processor until smooth and leave to cool. Whip the cream and mix in the yoghurt and blended fruit. Pour into individual glasses and decorate with chocolate shavings. Serve with shortbread fingers.

The yellow broom is waving abune the sunny brae,
And the rowan berries dancing where the sparkling waters play.

Lady John Scott, nineteenth century Scottish poet[30]

Clootie Dumpling (serves 10–12)

I was taught how to make clootie dumpling at a menu planning course in Falkirk College, Scotland. Black treacle is traditionally used but as it makes this quite a dark pudding, which I hate, I've substituted the treacle for golden syrup. This is traditionally made in a cloth (*cloot* in Scots, *claith* in Ulster-Scots). In Scotland, it is also traditional to serve it fried next morning for breakfast, with bacon and eggs!

Ingredients:

1lb/450g plain flour

6oz/170g white breadcrumbs

8oz/225g shredded suet

1 tsp baking powder

2 tsp cinnamon

2 tsp ginger

2 tsp mixed spice

4oz/115g glacé cherries

8oz/225g sultanas

8oz/225g raisins

8oz/225g soft brown sugar

8oz/225g golden syrup

2 eggs

2 Bramley apples, finely chopped

2 carrots, grated

2 lemon juice and rind

Preparation:

Use a clean white linen or cotton cloth (approximately 2ft/64cm square). Dampen with hot water and dust with plain flour and sugar, shaking off the excess.

Mix all the ingredients together in a large bowl, adding extra lemon juice if too dry. The mixture should be a soft dropping consistency. Pour onto the cloth, gather up the ends and tie with string, leaving room at the top for the mixture to expand. Pat into a round shape and place in a large pot filled with boiling water, with a saucer on the bottom to prevent the pudding from sticking. The water should come about two thirds up the pudding. Cover tightly with a lid and simmer gently for 3¾–4 hours. Top up with water if required.

Preheat the oven to 350°F, 180°C, Gas mark 4. Remove the pudding from the pan and dip it briefly into a sink filled with cold water to allow the cloth to come away easily from the skin. Remove the cloth and turn the pudding over onto an ovenproof plate. Place in the oven for 10–15 minutes or until the skin is shiny brown. Sprinkle with sugar and serve with custard and cream.

Wheaten Shortbread

Scotland is traditionally the home of shortbread. Most people already have a favourite plain shortbread recipe so this 'oaty' one makes a change.

Ingredients:

4oz/115g butter

1oz/30g plain flour

6oz/170g porridge oats

3oz/85g caster sugar

2oz/55g desiccated coconut

Pinch baking soda

Icing sugar for dusting

Preparation:

Cream the butter and sugar, and add the flour, oats, coconut and baking soda. Mix well and turn out onto a greased baking tray and press into the tin. Bake in a pre-heated oven at 325°F, 160°C, Gas mark 3 for approximately 20 minutes until golden. Dust with icing sugar while hot, and cut into squares.

Dundee Cake

The Scottish city of Dundee is famous for its marmalade and cake. Although Dundee Cake has been made in Scotland for centuries, it wasn't until the nineteenth century that a Scottish marmalade company made it commercially. The story goes that it was created especially for Mary, Queen of Scots, who wanted a fruit cake without the addition of cherries!

Ingredients:

8oz/225g plain flour

2tbsp ground almonds

1 tsp baking powder

5oz/140g caster sugar

5oz/140g soft margarine

3 large eggs

7oz/170g sultanas

7oz/170g raisins

Grated rind of lemon

Grated rind of orange

2oz/55g blanched almonds

Preparation:

Cream the margarine and sugar together. Whisk the eggs and add a little at a time to the mixture. Sift the flour and baking powder and fold into the mixture. Fold in the fruit, ground almonds and rinds. Pour the mixture into a greased round cake tin and decorate with blanched almonds. Bake in a pre-heated oven at 325°F, 170°C, Gas mark 3 for approximately 2 hours.

Tablet (Hard Fudge)

When I worked in a hotel in Scotland some years ago, we made traditional 'tablet' to serve to the guests after the Hogmanay meal. The end result should be a hard, grainy texture.

Ingredients:

1lb 12oz/800g caster sugar

6floz/170ml milk

6oz/170g unsalted butter

14oz/400g sweetened condensed milk

Preparation:

Put the milk and butter into a heavy based saucepan and stir until melted. Add the sugar and stir until dissolved. Add the condensed milk and stir continuously over a low heat until the mixture turns a light caramel shade (about 10 minutes). Don't let this bubble for too long or the end result will be a soft fudgy consistency which is what you don't want. Drop a small piece of the mixture into a cup of cold water and if it forms a small ball, then it's ready. Take off the heat, whisk it for a couple of minutes, then pour into a lightly oiled baking tray and leave to set in a cool place, before putting it into the fridge. When set, cut into 'tablets' or cubes.

Tipsy Sausages

This is an easy recipe for a finger buffet using whiskey and marmalade to marinate the sausages. It's a good idea to set out cocktail sticks so that guests can help themselves.

Ingredients:

1lb/450g Ulster Pork cocktail sausages
2 tbsp Bushmills Whiskey
6oz/170g Dundee orange marmalade

Preparation:

Put the marmalade into a large bowl and stir in the whiskey, mixing well until blended. Prick the sausages and add to the bowl, mixing until well coated in the marinade. Cover and leave overnight in the fridge, or for several hours, to allow the marinade to seep into the meat. Bake in a pre-heated oven at 400°F, 200°C or Gas mark 6 for 15–20 minutes until browned.

Bacon Proutas (Potatoes) with Soured Cream and Chive Dip

Another tasty recipe for a finger or hot buffet. The *proutas* also work well with a blue cheese or garlic dip.

Ingredients:

4 large potatoes

4 rashers of Ulster back bacon

Paprika, for dredging

Salt and pepper

Olive oil, for sprinkling

18fl oz/500ml soured cream

2oz/55g chives, finely chopped

Preparation:

Wash the potatoes, dry with kitchen paper, slice into wedges and place in large roasting dish. Sprinkle with oil, seasoning and paprika. Toss around until well mixed. Bake in a pre-heated oven at 400°F, 200°C, or Gas mark 6 for 20 minutes. Remove from the oven. Cut bacon into chunks and spread over potatoes. Return to oven for a further 20–25 minutes before serving.

Meanwhile, in a small bowl, mix the soured cream together with chives and serve with the proutas.

But leeze me on the precious Pratoe,
My country's stay!

James Orr, Bard of Ballycarry (1770–1816)[31]

Cheesy Mushroom and Onion Melts

Belfast Baps are traditionally huge round rolls and are excellent for hollowing out and filling with savoury food. This recipe uses onions, mushrooms and cheese and is a great alternative to a sandwich – but watch out – it's very filling!

Ingredients:

2 Belfast Baps, halved

4oz/115g Coleraine Cheddar, grated

8oz/225g mushrooms, sliced

1 small red onion, sliced thinly

1 clove garlic, peeled and crushed

Salt and pepper

2–3 tbsp olive oil

Parsley, chopped

Dash of Worcestershire sauce

Preparation:

Hollow out the baps and place on a lightly greased baking sheet. Brush with a little oil. Make crumbs from the hollowed out portion using a food processor or blender. Put 2 tbsp of oil into a pan and gently fry the onion and garlic until soft. Add the mushrooms, breadcrumbs, parsley, seasoning and sauce and cook for approximately 5 minutes. Fill the baps with the mixture and top with the cheese. Bake in a pre-heated oven at 400°F, 200°C, or Gas 6 for 7–10 minutes.

Moneyrea for baps 'n' tay,
Ballygowan for brandy,
Magherascouse for breedin' soos,
And Comber is the dandy.

Traditional County Down poem[32]

Soda Farl Carrickfergus

I created this in honour of the Carrickfergus Jailbreak of 1604! An Ayrshire Laird, Sir Hugh Montgomery, entered into a plan with his neighbour, Thomas Montgomery, a ship owner who traded regularly between Scotland and Carrickfergus. Sir Hugh persuaded Thomas to free the Gaelic Chieftain, Con O'Neill, from Carrickfergus Castle where he was imprisoned for waging war against Queen Elizabeth I in exchange for half of Con's lands in County Down. Thomas arrived in Carrickfergus in July, courted Annas Dobbin, the daughter of the town jailer in order to gain access to the castle, and smuggled a rope to Con, reputedly in a hollowed out cheese! Con was then able to scale the castle walls and escape to Scotland in Thomas' boat.

Ingredients:

2 soda farls (preferably homemade), halved horizontally

4oz/115g Coleraine Cheddar, thinly sliced

1 small tin chopped tomatoes, drained

Fresh basil, torn

Salt and pepper

Olive oil for sprinkling

Preparation:

Place the soda farls on a lightly greased baking sheet and spread with the tomatoes, basil and seasoning. Sprinkle with oil and top with the cheese slices. Bake in a pre-heated oven at 400°F, 200°C, Gas mark 6 for 7–10 minutes or until the cheese has melted over the sides of the farls.

There's some I'd share baith maut an' meal,
Nay, ee'n my penny fees wi',
But trust me lass, I'll ken them weel,
I'll share my bit o' cheese wi'.

Samuel Turner, Ballyclare (1804–1861)[33]

GLOSSARY OF FOOD AND FOOD TERMS

ULSTER-SCOTS	ENGLISH
aipple/epple	apple
becon	bacon
baket	baked
aboil	boiling
boul	bowl
breid	bread
butther	butter
coul	cold
coarn	corn
delft	crockery
bicker	cup
dännèr	dinner
däshes	dishes
deuck	duck
ait	eat
feesht	feast
fäsch	fish
flure	flour
graip	fork
gussgab	gooseberry
creesh	grease

gowpin	handful
hairst	harvest
het	hot
bonnock	oatcake
orkie	orchard
parritch	porridge
proota/pritta	potato
sup	sip
slae	sloe
broth	soup
steuch/steuchie	stew
strayberry	strawberry
boord	table
tay	tea
taypit	teapot
däshe-cloot	tea-towel
drooth	thirst
vinygar	vinegar
wätter/wathèr	water
wean	child
whaiten	wheaten

GLOSSARY OF WORDS AND PHRASES USED

ULSTER-SCOTS	ENGLISH
A blithe Yuletide an a guid Neu Yeir tae yin an aa!	A merry Christmas and a happy New Year to everyone!
brückly	dry, crumbly
claith	cloth
fadge	potato bread
Fair faa ye, yin an aa!	Hello/Welcome, everyone!
farl	a quarter piece
gaitherin	gathering, big event
gowpin	handful
Hairst	Harvest/Autumn
shooglin aboot	wobbling about
sup it up	drink or eat it up
tha De'il wull nab ye!	the Devil will get you!
tha slabbers wud be trippin' me	I'd be drooling
thran	stubborn
to mak yer teeth rin wätter	to make your mouth water
weans	children

BIBLIOGRAPHY

Ed. Adams, JRR and Robinson, PS, *The Country Rhymes of James Orr,* Bangor: Pretani Press, 1992

Ed. Adams, JRR and Robinson, PS, *The Country Rhymes of Samuel Thomson,* Bangor: Pretani Press, 1992

Brown, Catherine, *Classic Scots Cookery,* Glasgow: Angels' Share, 2004

Federation of Women's Institutes of Northern Ireland Cookery Book, undated

Fenton, James, *On Slaimish,* Belfast: Ullans Press, 2009

Fenton, James, *The Hamely Tongue (Revised Edition),* Belfast: Ullans Press, 2000

Ed. Hewitt, John, *Rhyming Weavers and Other Country Poets of Antrim and Down,* Belfast: Blackstaff Press, 2004

Lyons, David, *Scotland: Land of the Poets,* London: Promotional Reprint Co Ltd

Ed. Montgomery, Michael and Smyth, Anne, *A Blad o Ulster-Scotch frae Ullans,* Belfast: Ullans Press, 2003

Morrison, Allan, *Haud Yer Wheesht! – Your Scottish Granny's Favourite Sayings,* Glasgow: Neil Wilson Publishing Ltd, 1997

Robinson, Phillip, *Ulster-Scots: A Grammar of the Traditional Written and Spoken Language,* Belfast: Ullans Press, 1997

Ullans: the magazine for Ulster-Scots, Belfast: Ullans Press, various dates

REFERENCES

[1] Excerpt from Nicolson, Alexander (Scottish poet, nineteenth century), 'Skye', published in Lyons, David, *Scotland: Land of the Poets,* London: Promotional Reprint Co Ltd, 1996

[2] Anon, *A Scots Grace*

[3] Excerpt from Bruce, David (an Ulster-Scot-American poet c.1760–1830), *A 'CANNY WORD' to the Democrats of the West*

[4] Excerpt from Morrison, Allan, *Haud Yer Wheesht! – Your Scottish Granny's Favourite Sayings,* Glasgow: Neil Wilson Publishing Ltd, 1997

[5] Excerpt from Starratt, William, *An Elegy on the Much-Lamented Death of Quarter-master Brice Blair*

[6] *My Aunt Jane* (Traditional)

[7] Excerpt from Morrison, Allan, *Haud Yer Wheesht! – Your Scottish Granny's Favourite Sayings,* Glasgow: Neil Wilson Publishing Ltd, 1997

[8] Excerpt from Morrison, Allan, *Haud Yer Wheesht! – Your Scottish Granny's Favourite Sayings,* Glasgow: Neil Wilson Publishing Ltd, 1997

[9] Excerpt from McDonald Flecher, Henry (Bard of Ballinderry, 1827 –?), 'The Churn', published in Ed. Hewitt, John, *Rhyming Weavers and Other Country Poets of Antrim and Down,* Belfast: Blackstaff Press, 2004

[10] Excerpt from Morrison, Allan, *Haud Yer Wheesht! – Your Scottish Granny's Favourite Sayings,* Glasgow: Neil Wilson Publishing Ltd, 1997

[11] Excerpt from Porter, Hugh (Bard of Moneyslane, 1781–?), 'Hospitality', published in Ed. Hewitt, John, *Rhyming Weavers and Other Country Poets of Antrim and Down,* Belfast: Blackstaff Press, 2004

12 Fenton, James, 'The Epple-Tree', in *On Slaimish*, Belfast: Ullans Press, 2009

13 Excerpt from Hogg, James (Scottish poet, 1770–1835), 'McLean's Welcome', published in Lyons, David, *Scotland: Land of the Poets*, London: Promotional Reprint Co Ltd, 1996

14 Excerpt from Starratt, William, *An Elegy on the Much-Lamented Death of Quarter-master Brice Blair*

15 Excerpt from Herbison, David (The Bard of Dunclug, 1800–1880), 'The Auld Wife's Lament for her Teapot', published in Ed. Hewitt, John, *Rhyming Weavers and Other Country Poets of Antrim and Down*, Belfast: Blackstaff Press, 2004

16 *Achanee, whun A was wee* (Traditional)

17 Excerpt from Sloan, Edward L (Bard of Conlig, 1800s), 'Halloween', published in Ed. Hewitt, John, *Rhyming Weavers and Other Country Poets of Antrim and Down*, Belfast: Blackstaff Press, 2004

18 *Sausages in the pan* (Traditional)

19 *Jelly on the plate* (Traditional)

20 *Up Hard Breid Raa* (Traditional)

21 Excerpt from Thomson, Samuel (Bard of Carngranny, 1766–1816), 'An Epistle', published in Ed. Hewitt, John, *Rhyming Weavers and Other Country Poets of Antrim and Down*, Belfast: Blackstaff Press, 2004

22 Excerpt from 'TIT for TAT: or the Rater rated: A new song, in Way of Dialogue, between a Laggen farmer and his Wife', part of Anon, *'Scotch Poems' from East Donegal in 1753*

23 Excerpt from Gillen, Charlie, 'Mackerel', in *Ullans: the magazine for Ulster-Scots*, Belfast: Ullans Press, No 9 and 10, Winter 2004

24 Excerpt from Donnelly, Robert (nineteenth century), 'To a Linen Manufacturer', Ed. Hewitt, John, *Rhyming Weavers and Other Country Poets of Antrim and Down,* Belfast: Blackstaff Press, 2004

25 *Did you treat your Mary Ann* (Traditional)

26 Excerpt from Huddleston, Robert (Bard of Moneyreagh, 1800s), 'The Lammas Fair (Belfast)', published in Ed. Hewitt, John, *Rhyming Weavers and Other Country Poets of Antrim and Down,* Belfast: Blackstaff Press, 2004

27 *Christmas is coming* (Traditional)

28 Excerpt from Gillen, Charlie, 'Pratas', in *Ullans: the magazine for Ulster-Scots,* Belfast: Ullans Press, No 9 and 10, Winter 2004

29 Excerpt from Thomson, Samuel (Bard of Carngranny, 1766–1816), 'Simkin, or a Bargain's a Bargain – a Tale', published in Ed. Adams, JRR and Robinson, PS, *The Country Rhymes of Samuel Thomson,* Bangor: Pretani Press, 1992

30 Excerpt from Scott, Lady John (Scottish poet, nineteenth century), 'Durisdeer', published in Lyons, David, *Scotland: Land of the Poets,* London: Promotional Reprint Co Ltd, 199

31 Excerpt from Orr, James (Bard of Ballycarry, 1770–1816), 'To The Potatoe', published in Ed. Adams, JRR and Robinson, PS, *The Country Rhymes of James Orr,* Bangor: Pretani Press, 1992

32 *Moneyrea for baps 'n' tay* (Traditional)

33 Excerpt from Turner, Samuel (1804–1861), *Lines sent to Mrs IGF on Receipt of a Present of Cheese*

INDEX

PICTURE CREDITS

All photographs by the author and her family except for the following which are included with kind permission of the copyright holders:

iStockphoto: page 18, (right column, second from top)

Jeremy Keith: page 18 (left column, top)

Waddell Media: page 9

The image on page 18 (left column, top) is licensed under the Creative Commons Attribution 2.0 Generic License. Permission is granted to share and/or remix this work providing the work is attributed in the manner specified by the author or licensor. A copy of this license can be viewed at http://creativecommons.org/licenses/by/2.0/

Copyright has been acknowledged to the best of our ability. If there are any inadvertent errors or omissions, we shall be happy to correct them in any future editions.